G000162964

MIDGET CAR RACING

MIDGET CAR RACING

BELLE VUE SPEEDWAY
1934-39

DEREK BRIDGETT

FONTHILL

This book is dedicated to the late Dave Gandhi. In the late thirties, as a precocious teenager, he attended every Midget Car meeting that took place at Belle Vue speedway; he even managed to ingratiate himself with the management and gain admittance to all those areas that the general public were not allowed to enter. His many anecdotes and stories gave a unique insight into the 'behind the scenes' activity of the track.

The late Dave Ghandi proudly wearing his Stoke Potters Supporters' Club badge.

Fonthill Media Limited
Fonthill Media LLC
www.fonthillmedia.com
office@fonthillmedia.com

First published in the United Kingdom 2013
British Library Cataloguing in Publication Data:
A catalogue record for this book is available from the British Library
Copyright © Derek Bridgett 2013

ISBN 978-1-78155-240-7

The right of Derek Bridgett to be identified as the author of this work has been asserted by him in accordance with the Copyright, Designs and Patents Act 1988.
All rights reserved. No part of this publication may be reproduced, stored in a retrieval system or transmitted in any form or by any means, electronic, mechanical, photocopying, recording or otherwise, without prior permission in writing from Fonthill Media Limited

Typeset in 10 pt/13 pt Sabon
Printed and bound in England

Contents

Preface

In the early sixties I was fortunate enough to be allowed into that holy of holies; the pits at Belle Vue speedway. Parked underneath the wooden grandstand and peeping from underneath an old tarpaulin sheet were some weird-looking racing cars. Quite why these cars were there was a mystery and what they had been used for was an even bigger puzzle. The cars looked as though they were something to do with the nearby fun fair. Maybe they were surplus to requirements, a redundant ride that was no longer attracting thrill seekers, or perhaps they were there for repair? Other than a cursory glance there was never enough time to investigate them further.

Fast forward forty plus years to the opening of the Rockingham Motor Speedway in May 2001 and the mystery was solved. Parked amongst a static exhibition of British Oval racing cars, and sitting between a Ford V8-60 engined midget car and a Kurtis midget car was a small racing car that looked exactly like the cars that were abandoned underneath the grandstand all those years ago. In front of the car was an information board which stated that the car was a 1936 ELTO 4-60, and had raced at Belle Vue speedway in the nineteen thirties. Now that the identity of the Belle Vue cars had been established more intriguing questions needed to be answered; where did they come from, when were they raced, who drove them and how did one similar to those first seen under the grandstand end up on display at Rockingham? A long protracted search now began in which to find out more about Midget Car racing at Belle Vue speedway, especially the pre-war period. The search was to prove a lot more difficult than was first envisaged.

With Midget cars sharing the same track and stadium as Manchester's Belle Vue motorcycle speedway team there shouldn't have been too much of a problem. After all there is a huge amount of information available about this famous speedway team, as there is about the majority of other British speedway teams. All the newspapers of the time devoted vast amounts of column inches to (as it was called at the time) dirt track racing; and speedway historians have collated and published the results of practically every race that took place. There are even magazines devoted entirely to the past glories of speedway and also several books have been written about individual tracks. How wrong I was! For some reason or another Midget Car Speedway racing had been ignored except by a handful of devotees. It was a similar story with the 'main stream' motor racing press; Midget Car racing was discounted. Occasionally there

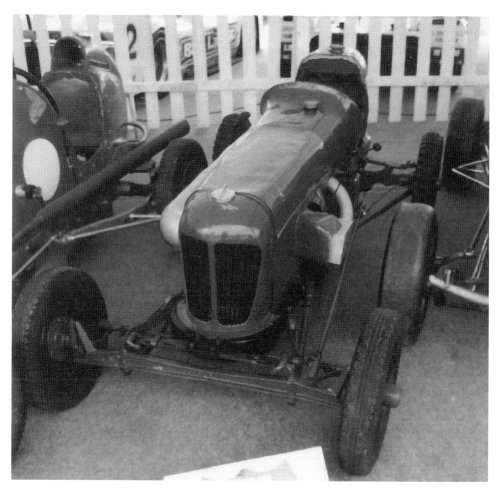

The Elto 4/60 on display at Rockingham Motor Speedway's inaugural meeting.

were a few terse columns but no seriousness reporting nor depth to the articles. When a car designed for the speedway tracks did participate at the Shelsley Walsh hill climb, the magazine *Motor Sport* critically reported, 'Shelsley is not a circus'.

Luckily there were several families in the north west whose relatives raced these little cars. Together with their help it became possible to answer all the questions posed when the Elto reappeared on the scene. Thankfully they had kept many photographs, programmes and press cuttings all of which proved to be invaluable. With the aid of this memorabilia several dates could be established which led to the meagre reports that appeared in the regional newspapers of the time. In due course all the information came together and I was able to make sense of the pre-war history of oval car racing at Manchester's famous Belle Vue stadium.

Chapter 1

Cars and Bikes

'See the pick of the World's Best Drivers Racing All out for the Belle Vue Grand Prix', seemed an odd and unusual statement to make in a national newspaper that was published on 9 August 1938. However there was nothing odd or unusual about the huge crowd that witnessed the racing. On the night of 10 August they saw Walter Mackereth walk away with the Grand Prix trophy. All of the above might seem a tad confusing to the students of Motor Racing history. The Belle Vue that the advert was referring to was not some exotic location on the Cote D'Azur but a thrirty-five-acre site at Longsite, South Manchester! They would certainly never have heard of Walter Mackereth nor would they believe that a Motor Racing Grand Prix would have taken place at a venue named Belle Vue. For a start those folk who don't live in the north west of England would wonder where Belle Vue was; others would ask what sort of a motor race meeting could have taken place in Manchester in 1938. The Belle Vue that the advert was referring to was a purpose built oval speedway track that was constructed in a corner of the north-west's premier theme park at Hyde Road.

The first mention of Belle Vue as a 'theme park' goes as far back as the 1830s, when an advert appeared in the *Manchester Guardian* which read '...the Belle Vue Gardens...are now open...' Over the years a zoo and an aviary were developed, and later a boating lake, a pleasure park and an extensive fun fair. During the first fifty years of the twentieth century this fun fair was to boast some of the most fearsome fairground rides in the country. All sorts of side shows were introduced –including (believe it or not) a flea circus! Large halls were constructed on the site, which played host to a traditional circus, championship boxing tournaments, professional wrestling, brass band concerts and other popular events. Finally in 1928 the greatest speedway track ever to be constructed in Britain was added to the attractions, around this track was built several covered seated grandstands. Records show that that the wide 418-yard (382-m) dirt track oval opened on Saturday 23 March. The stadium and track were built to cash in on the latest motorcycle craze that was sweeping the country. This new form of motorcycle dirt track racing had its origins in Australia and was allegedly introduced to the British public in February 1928 at High Beach, Hertfordshire. A date hotly disputed by many of the north-west's motorcycle historians who claim that the first motorcycle dirt-track held in the UK was actually held eight months earlier at Droylsden on 25 June 1927. It was the height of the 'roaring twenties' and from the start

Lurid newspaper advertisements appeared regularly in the local press.

dirt track racing was an absolute sensation. The race meetings were part showmanship part motor sport and perfect entertainment for the times. The British public flocked in their tens of thousands to witness this new phenomenon. Almost every town in the UK had its own track, many of them built inside existing Greyhound tracks. By the end of 1929 there were at least four speedway tracks operating in the Manchester area; the White City greyhound stadium, the Albion stadium Salford, Kirkmanshulme Lane greyhound stadium, which was at the other end of the Belle Vue 'theme park' and a separate commercial entity altogether. And finally there was the track that was without doubt the finest of them all, Belle Vue. The track was purpose built and as such it didn't have to make any compromises. There was no need to fit a track inside a greyhound track or around an existing sports facility. It was this track that was to become the home of the Belle Vue 'Aces' motorcycle speedway team, a team that was to dominate the British speedway League right up until the outbreak of the Second World War.

To oversee the first and subsequent further meetings was Belle Vue employee Eric Oliver Spence. Throughout his managerial career he was always referred to as E. O. Spence or simply EO. It was Spence who saw to it that that this new venture was viable and profitable. Through his flair and showmanship he made the track a commercial success. It was on this magnificent track those eight years after the opening meeting that Walter Mackereth won the Belle Vue Grand Prix. The popularity of motorcycle speedway racing in Manchester cannot be overstated; crowds flocked to the track to see the riders send up showers of cinders as they broadsided their mounts around the bends. Originally all dirt track races were individual events and a variety of races were held. There were heats and finals, match races between two riders and all kinds of record attempts; these could be anything from one lap to four laps. There was even an event called the Lancashire mile. Promoters had to think up various types of novelties to keep the paying public wanting to come back for more. When attendances started to wane team races were tagged on to the main events, and eventually team racing became the most popular. This was a shrewd move by the promoters as team racing created a loyal fan base. These partisan fans could not only cheer on their favourite rider but also get behind their team. In fact team racing was to be the mainstay of British motorcycle speedway right up to the present day. Once the boom was over the other Manchester tracks faded away leaving Belle Vue the premier speedway stadium, not only in Manchester but also in the North West.

With bikes tearing around the dirt track ovals it wouldn't be long before the question would be asked, how would cars perform on the dirt tracks? Tradition has it that the first track to stage oval dirt track racing for cars in the UK was on the half-mile trotting track at Greenford. This event took place on 23 June 1928 and was organised by the Junior Car Club who were responsible for many of the prestigious events held at the famous Brooklands race track. It is hard to judge whether this event was a success or not; there was plenty of publicity, a good crowd and a sympathetic report in the motoring press. Seeing as this was the one and only meeting to take place there it might not have been as popular as the organisers had wished. In the South of England the proximity of Brooklands probably hampered any further ventures into dirt track racing, as no matter what type of racing was presented it was always going to be compared to the Weybridge track. In the North West there were no such problems. Wanting to see what the cars could do on the dirt at least, three tracks decided to experiment with this type of racing. Members of the go ahead Huddersfield Motor Club embraced the dirt tracks, putting on demonstrations at the Thrum Hall track Halifax, their home track at Huddersfield and the exciting half-mile oval trotting track at Highfield Road Blackpool. The Blackpool experiment ended uncomfortably for the organisers as one of the competitors was seriously injured when his car turned over and crashed into the perimeter fence. This accident seemed to dent any further enthusiasm for car racing on the dirt.

So far the cars had only raced against one another. After seeing cars race on the track there was one obvious question being asked, which was, what would win in a race between a car and a bike? The ever astute Spence spotted an opportunity to publicise his track. By staging such an event he would be keeping Belle Vue well in the public eye. From the two-wheeled side of the challenge Spence could call on any number of his motorcycle speedway stars plus other riders from around the area. Choosing a car to race against the bikes might prove a little more difficult, especially one that could put up a decent performance. The cars that had competed at Blackpool and at the other tracks were just stripped down sports tourers. If the car was to stand a chance then a fast single-seated racing car was needed. Spence was fortunate in this respect as just south of Manchester at nearby Macclesfield a certain Basil Davenport had built and raced such a fast single seat machine. This car, known as the 'Spider', was to become

Basil Davenports' 'Spider' still competes successfully in the twenty-first century.

a legend in the hands of Davenport. By June 1930 it was the fastest British car up the famous Shelsley Walsh Hill Climb, and over eighty years later it is still competing very successfully in Vintage Hill Climb events. Davenport's 'Spider' was ideal for dirt track racing as it was light and consisted of nothing more than a simple chassis, seat and a powerful air-cooled 1,500cc V-twin engine. But what made it more suitable than conventional racing cars was that it was chain driven, with a fixed differential drive (i.e. both wheels had equal drive). With both rear wheels gripping the loose surface of the Belle Vue track it was a perfect set up. Rather than race against the bikes straight away, Davenport was invited along to exhibit the car and to assess whether or not the car would be competitive. Saturday 20 September 1930 was the date set aside for the trial. Belle Vue advertised the event in the local paper as, 'new sensation B. Davenport will try out and demonstrate The "Spider" 130 MPH Car'. Also on the bill that night was a match race between Frank Varey and Eric Langton, both mounted on their special speedway Scott motorcycles. There was also the *Evening Chronicle* Cup, a solo competition for the Silver Helmet and the third round of a 'Broadsiding' competition, which was probably a pre-cursor of our modern drifting competitions, except for bikes and not cars. Basil's demonstration must have been impressive as the following week, Saturday 27 September, he was booked to race against one of the top motorcycle speedway riders in the North West; the rider chosen was Walter Hull. Walter was not based at the Belle Vue track but at Manchester's other leading track; Old Trafford's White City Stadium. The car versus bike was the climax of the evening's entertainment being the last event on the programme. Walter had had a successful night having won every race in which he had competed. In the match race he was again mounted aboard his special dirt track Douglas bike. Hull and Davenport did their warm up laps and were ready for the rolling start; Hull leapt into the lead and despite having only 500cc against Davenport's 1,500 he won the race. As the *Manchester Guardian* wrote Hull had, 'settled an argument by beating Basil Davenport'. After that nothing more was heard of cars appearing on the Hyde Road Track.

Because of the success of motorcycle speedway racing a few motor racing enthusiasts felt that there might, after all, be a future for cars racing on speedway tracks. The following year, 1931, one or two cars were under construction all with a view to racing on the dirt tracks. Alan Kilfoyle, a West Ham based speedway rider, came up with a small car he called 'The Yellow Peril'! As far as it is known this car only ever gave one demonstration. This was supposed to be at West Ham on 23 June 1931. In the North of England a certain Mr Treganza of Brighouse Yorkshire built a special car in which he hoped to challenge all comers. None of these cars are recorded as having turned up at Manchester. One of the specials that did turn up at Manchester was built by Doug Copley. Doug made the trip from his home base in Birmingham to test the machine. This was a rather flimsy car powered by a front engine V-twin. Later in the year a few other well-known motor racing drivers tried their luck at the famous Wembley Stadium. Of those that rolled up that night were, Mrs Tommy Wisdom, H. J. Aldington and R. G. H. Nash. Of these the fastest was Nash who ended up borrowing a fellow competitor's car when his own car, 'The Terror', developed supercharger trouble. Nash trundled around in 24 seconds. He returned later on 22 October taking 'The Terror'

The Dirt Track car that Treganza built to challenge all comers.

around in 22.2 seconds. This time was to remain unbeaten for five years! It was not until 1936 that this time was bettered by up and coming Midget Car driver Walter Mackereth. The car that Nash drove was from the Frazer-Nash workshops. It was well sorted, well prepared and perfectly suited to the dirt tracks; its differential-less rear axle entirely suited to power sliding on the cinders. For the cars to have any sort of impact on the dirt ovals more competitive cars were needed. Unfortunately there was never enough around for promoters or spectators to take them seriously. The anticipated surge for car speedway on dirt ovals never materialised.

The few cars that were available could only give demonstrations and challenge track records that they had previously made. Several track record attempts were tried, from one lap to one mile. Once a time had been set up speedway promoters could invite other drivers along to break these records. This gave the promoters a new novelty event with which to fill their programme. It was not until 1933 that Belle Vue decided to establish records for cars.

Once again the Belle Vue management hadn't far to look for a suitable car and driver. Manchester boasted the well-respected coach-building firm of Arnold's, who produced bespoke bodies for Rolls-Royce and other top of the range cars. The son of the firm's owners, Allen Arnold, was a racing car enthusiast and by 1933 owned a quick Frazer-Nash single-seat racing car. Arnold's car had been previously owned by R. G. S. Nash of Wembley track record fame and in actual fact it was the same car, 'The Terror' that held the Wembley one lap record. Arnold's record attempt was set for 5 August. That night there was a varied programme of events; a supporter's trophy race, a match race and several record attempts. Apart from Arnold, Max Grosskreutz (the great Australian speedway rider and later promoter) was out to attack the one

'The Terror' recently purchased by
Allen Arnold in 1932.

lap motorcycle record, and Eric Langton attempted the four lap standing start. When
the meeting was advertised in the *Manchester Guardian* the main headline read,
'Sensational Car Lap Record attempt by Allen Arnold, in a Frazer-Nash Car, The
Terror, capacity 120mph'. This is a rather odd statement which appears to emphasise
the gulf between motorcycle speedway and car racing. To get the top speed and the
engine capacity mixed up was typical of the divide. Arnold was determined to put on a
good show. His car had proven ability on the dirt, but Arnold wanted to make the car
even more competitive on the loose surface of the dirt track. Grip and drive were the
key factors on the dirt. To improve the grip Arnold fitted twin rear wheels to the back
of the car and also fitted these rear wheels with the same tyres as those used on the
speedway bikes. After the bikes had completed their programmed events, Arnold took
to the track. His time was six and one fifths seconds slower than the time speedway
rider Eric Langton had set the previous month. Arnold's time might not have seemed
too bad, but one has to take into account that Langton's time was set from a standing
start! A rolling start could knock at least one second off the time. The cars still had a
long way to go before they came anywhere near the times that the bikes were setting.

Nevertheless Arnold's feat must have impressed those that mattered. Two weeks
later it was decided to invite along a different driver/car combination to assail the four
lap record. Unlike the South of England there were no metal surfaced racetracks in the
North. What the North West did have was a huge expanse of hard flat sand between

The big Bugatti being tested around the Hyde Road track.

The long tail had been deliberately bobbed to avoid scuffing the safety fence.

Formby and Southport. The local motor clubs made full use of this gift of nature. They organised race meetings on various tracks that were laid out on the wide beach. One of the North West's star competitors on the sand was Southport's Jack Field. Jack owned an extremely fast 2.3 single seat Bugatti that had was once owned by Malcolm Campbell. In this car Jack excelled on the loose surface, and there are many photographs of him sliding his car sideways as he powered around the turns. Naturally this caught the eye of the Belle Vue management, so it was no surprise that they invited him along to challenge the time set by Allan Arnold. The Bugatti was considerably longer than Arnold's Frazer-Nash. This extra length could well have proved an encumbrance on the narrower Belle Vue speedway track. Being a conventional racing car the Bugatti had a long streamlined tail that extended well beyond the rear axle line. If Field's car got into a long broadside and drifted too close to the perimeter fence then there was a good chance that the tail would come into contact with the fence! Field foresaw this problem and had the tail chopped off, Manx style. This meant that the end of the car finished just behind the rear wheels. Despite the cosmetic tweaks and the extra power of the Bugatti, Field was unable to better Arnold's time. After this attempt nothing more was heard about cars attacking track records. Cars did turn up again on 23 September when there was a match race between a 1903 American Overland buckboard motorcar and a DeDion. Today, great respect would be given to these veteran cars, but back in 1933 the crowd treated the old crocks with much derision.

Chapter 2

Early Demonstrations

It was events in the South of England and in the United States in particular that led to Midget Car Racing arriving at the Hyde Road track. As far back as 1932, a certain Jean Reville of Wimbledon had set out to try and popularise car racing on speedway tracks. He realised that publicity was the key to winning over the public. One headline grabber would be to introduce a woman racing driver to the tracks. One lady who would relish such a challenge was Faye Taylour. Faye was well known around the speedway tracks having raced bikes all over the country before the inevitable ban on lady speedway riders. Wembley jumped at the chance to put on a match race between Reville and Taylour. Taylour was to drive an Alto and Reville a special front wheel drive BSA-based car of his own construction. All the publicity and hype in the world could not disguise the fact that the racing wasn't very good. The press for a change weren't taken in by the propaganda; they were honest enough to report, 'these shows do not excite the huge crowds of spectators as the motorcycles do'.

Over in the United States a new type of motor racing was taking off, which catered for little cars and suited small ovals perfectly. Reville may well have known what was happening across the Atlantic. In this country he set out to prove the sceptics wrong and that his vision of small racing cars on dirt ovals had a place on the UK's speedway tracks. He went on to develop small single-seat racing cars suitable for the short oval tracks. Once he had built enough cars of his own, and had persuaded a few other motor racing enthusiast to join him, he negotiated a deal with the owners of the Crystal Palace to present Midget Car speedway on their oval dirt track. The first all car meeting took place on Saturday 30 March 1934. The meeting must have gone down well as further meetings solely for cars took place there throughout the rest of 1934.

Always with an eye for the main chance the Belle Vue management invited Reville along to show case his cars. Three cars came up from London to show off their paces in a series of match races. Apart from Reville himself the two other rivals were Leon Marret and Victor Gillow. By now all three of them were reasonably experienced at racing on oval dirt tracks. Revile and Marrat were to drive Palmer specials, both of which had been built at Reville's workshops. The little cars were very lightweight and used parts taken from front wheel drive BSAs. Gillows' car, on the other hand, was much more orthodox. It was basically a stripped down Brooklands Riley; and as such had the engine in the front conventionally driving the rear wheels.

A full colour programme cover was produced for Crystal Palaces' first Midget Car Meeting.

Saturday 12 May was the chosen day. Great excitement was generated in the press as lurid adverts showed cars that were similar to those that were to race in Manchester crashing into the safety fence. The most dramatic publicity photo appeared in the Northern edition of the National Daily Newspapers. The photo was allegedly taken during a practice session and showed one of the cars lying on its side. The driver has been thrown out and is lying unconscious nearby as another car passes him by! To the naked eye this shot showed how dangerous and spectacular this new form of motor racing could be. Closer examination of the photo might suggest that it was a staged photo especially set up for the press. It is doubtful if the press photographers of the time had the equipment or the knowledge of where to stand to capture such a moment.

On the night a reported crowd of 30,000 spectators lined the terraces. This could have been due to the added attraction of the cars, but it was more likely because motorcycle speedway was so popular in Manchester. After the speedway riders had completed their scheduled events it was the turn of the cars to show just why they were so popular at London's Crystal Palace track. Early in the first race Reville and Marrat had a 'coming to-gether', but after quickly sorting themselves out, Marret went on to win in unspectacular fashion. The other races proved to be just as dull and slow. None of the drivers were able to get anywhere near the time set by Allen Arnold the previous year. The big crowd didn't find the racing exciting; the buzz around the stadium was that car racing would not appeal in the North of England. The *Manchester Guardian* claimed that, '...the track was too narrow to allow the drivers to show much of their

The first of the many dramatic Midget Car advertisements that appeared in the Manchester Journals.

Belle Vue regularly fabricated publicity stunts.

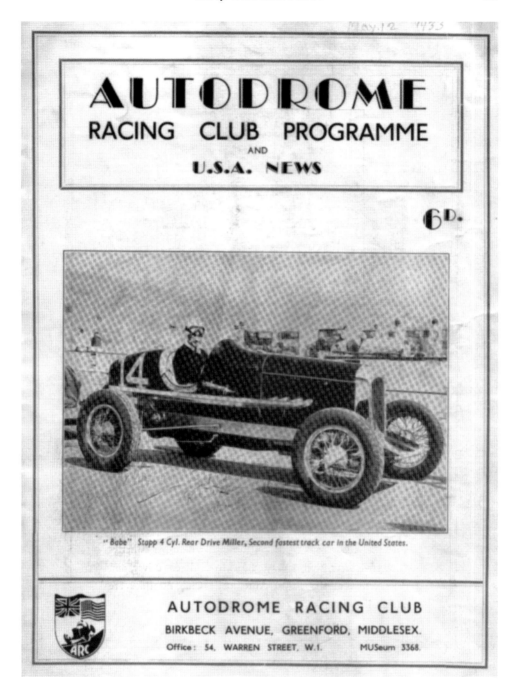

The US influence is evident on the cover of the Greenford programme.

skill or the capacity of their cars'. Much the same was written in the other northern dailies. Thus the attempt to cash in on the success that the cars were having in London was a failure.

Manchester may not have been ready to embrace car speedway but in the south of England it was certainly a different story. Crystal Palace continued to play to big audiences. Greenford had reopened on 5 May and ran two meetings, both under the guidance of one of midget car racing's most charismatic figures, Spike Rhiando. Mr Rhiando's approach was a little different because the drivers and the cars that competed there were all regular participants at Brooklands so they had to comply with the rules and regulations that were laid down by the RAC. Later in the year further meetings took place in London. When motorcycle speedway ceased at the Lea Bridge track midget car racing took over; and in the autumn of the same year Brighton opened for a short season.

Chapter 3

Midget Cars Make their Debut

At the start of 1935 no one knew, or perhaps didn't really care, what the future of Midget Car Racing was to be in the UK. Over in the United States it was a different story. Legend has it that the first Midget Car Race took place at Hughes Stadium, Sacramento in July 1933. Ever since that inaugural meeting Midget Car Racing had gone from strength to strength and is still flourishing today. After the initial meeting other venues quickly opened up and this innovative and unusual form of motor racing spread further down the west coast, before crossing into the mid-west. It then swept to the east coast before finally reaching the south. By 1935 there wasn't a state in the country that wasn't presenting Midget Car Racing. One of the most surprising aspects of this extraordinary growth was that it developed during the depths of The Great Depression. America was going through the worst economic crisis that the world had ever known, and the people were desperate and would do anything to make a buck. There had been many creative ideas, most of which came to nothing; fortunately Midget Car Racing was not one of them. The desperation of those tough years had spawned a new form of reasonably cheap motor racing that was to reach every continent in the world.

Seeing how the sport had taken off in the United States it was felt, in certain quarters at least, that it would be only a matter of time before the UK too would take to Midget Car Racing. Reville believed that this would soon happen but his cars and presentations had not quite broken through into the big time. As one of the managers of a huge entertainment complex it was Spence's job to look out for new and novel forms of enjoyment. The continual search for thrill seeking attractions would keep Belle Vue in the vanguard of entertainment thus ensuring that it would continue to be the 'playground of the North'. Hearing about reports coming from the USA Spence sensed another profit-making opportunity. With the correct cars and favourable publicity he could take UK Midget Car Racing to the same heights that were currently being enjoyed in America. The big problem was trying to find cars that could perform as well as the bikes. The cars that were competing in 1934 were not really up to the job. In the London area the challenge of constructing a suitable car been taken up by Jean Reville and his partner Arthur Palmer. They abandoned their converted BSA-based cars and concentrated on constructing a small lightweight single-seater car. The little car they built was much more suitable for short circuit racing. Their new creation gained lots of

Jean Revile courted publicity by claiming that the *Gnat* was the world's smallest Racing Car.

publicity as it was described as the world's smallest car. It gained even more exposure when it was put on display at Olympia where the Jubilee exhibition was taking place.

If Spence wanted to emulate the success of the US Midgets he needed to encourage the building of proper midget cars much like the car Reville had constructed. Once there were enough decent cars around then there was just a chance that the public would take an interest in them. His idea was to encourage enthusiasts to build their own cars. To coax eager constructors to come forward he wrote several articles in the *Belle Vue Bulletin*; which was a programme come magazine that was on sale at every motorcycle speedway meeting. The most inspiring article he wrote stated, 'anyone who has a real Midget Car and needs the opportunity of trying it out on the speedway had better come along to Belle Vue. We shall be pleased to give them every possible facility. To help men who want to be in on this sport we have formed a club here at Belle Vue. Mechanics will have access to a pool of practical technical information on specifications and construction. Whether they buy or build cars they will have expert advice, and when the vehicles are an established fact they will become proficient on the track. The cost of building such a car should be about £100-£150.' Obviously progress depended on the right sort of car; it was now up to the local car devotees to come up with the goods. A serious attempt was now being made; as Spence suggested in another of his press releases he wanted to give the public the, '"REAL THING" and nothing but the real thing right from the start'. The cut down roadsters and sports cars would no longer do.

In early 1935 the population of UK was planning the Silver Jubilee celebrations of King George V and Queen Mary. Festivities were to be held throughout the country. On the day set aside for Jubilee Day, Monday 6 May, Belle Vue speedway was to stage its biggest ever celebratory meeting. They advertised the fact that no money or effort would be spared on putting on a bumper programme. It was said that apart from the England versus Australia speedway Test matches, this was to be the most expensive event ever staged. To boost the motorcycle speedway programme Midget Cars were to appear in the line-up. Instead of giving demonstrations or match races, a series of races between suitable cars was to take place. To boost interest even further, Belle Vue's top speedway riders were to try their luck at Midget Car Racing. They were to race against several of the south's proven Midget Car drivers. One race on the bill that the local supporters were looking forward to was a special race between Belle Vue's top rider, Frank Varey and Londoner Les White. At the start of the year for some unknown reason, Frank had decided to retire from motorcycle speedway racing. The magazine *Light Car* said, 'Frank Varey, idol of the Belle Vue motorcycle fans is quitting two wheels for four. Lots more, they tell me, are soon to follow suit'. The last quote was rather optimistic as no one did follow Frank's example, in fact Frank changed his mind and made a sensational come back. After his 'retirement' he returned to ride even better for the 'Aces'. Frank's opponent, Wembley-based Les White, had fabricated his own Salmson powered Midget; this driver car combination was getting better with every outing. Building on his past experiences Les had quickly developed his race craft, and

Les White was an employee of the British Salmson car company and he used one of their engines to power his home-built special. (Courtesy of Malcolm White)

The Gillow Riley was the top car in 1935.

his Salmson Special was now one of the best Midgets on the track. Frank's mount was a Gillow Riley Special. Victor Gillow was a well-known Riley exponent who had had considerable success road racing. He was now converting this road racing success to the dirt ovals. In the true sense of the word the Gillow Special wasn't exactly a Midget car, but a small driver-car converted for the dirt. At the time Gillow and his Special were without doubt the best combination at the Crystal Palace track.

One or two local constructors had answered Spence's call to build suitable cars. By the time the Jubilee meeting came around none of the cars under construction were deemed ready enough to take part. After the bikes had put on their usual fast exciting racing it was the turn of the invited cars. The speedway fans were particularly looking forward to seeing how their favourite rider Frank Varey would perform. Frank didn't let them down, in a special four lap rolling start match race, he led home Les White in the rather slow time of 1 minute 30 2/5 seconds. Despite a year's development the cars hadn't set Manchester alight. The times were at least TEN seconds slower than the bikes. Furthermore when four cars were put on the track together the times were even worse and the racing impossible.

Nineteen days after the Jubilee meeting the fastest car ever to grace the Hyde Road track did a few laps. It wasn't that Spence and the car constructers had come up with

The extra publicity generated by the Bluebird exhibition encouraged more people to visit Belle Vue's theme park.

How Belle Vue's resident cartoonist would have liked to have seen the victorious Speedway team perform their lap of honour.

an amazing new speedy machine; on the contrary the car in question was towed slowly around the circuit behind the tracks' tractor. The sensational car was in fact Sir Malcolm Campbell's latest land speed creation *Bluebird*. For the past few days the car had been on display in the pleasure gardens, so it was only natural that the management wanted to get as much publicity out of its visit as possible. By towing it around the track they were able to show off their latest attraction to even more people.

After the poor performance of the cars at the Jubilee meeting, most promoters would have abandoned the idea of Midget Car racing. Spence took a different view and encouraged the locals to redouble their efforts. The lessons they had learned from watching the London-based cars were taken on board and implemented in the construction of their latest creations. To show that progress was being made Spence regularly invited along influential reporters, and these journalists attended the frequent practice sessions that were now taking place. Better reports were coming from the tracks at Crystal Palace and Lea Bridge. Due to the improvement in Midget Car design there had been an increase in speed and reliability. Spence believed that the cars that were now being used were at about the same stage of development as the speedway bikes had been five years previously. In those five years speedway bikes had change from being converted sports models to specialist machines. They now had light-weight frames, specialist tyres and all most ninety-nine per cent were powered by the ubiquitous 500cc speedway JAP engine. As a result of these developments speed and reliability had rocketed. Spence and his group of enthusiastic specialist motor engineers began to build on the lessons learned from the speedway boys.

By July the locals had their cars ready. Saturday 27 July was the date set aside to give the cars one last chance to prove their viability. If they hadn't improved this time then there was a distinct chance that Midget Car Racing would just become another sideshow. On the day chosen all the best and most interesting Midgets in the UK were to take part, as well as the best of the locally-built models. A large assembly of cars and drivers from the South were to pit their vehicles against one another plus a couple of cars from Manchester. The local cars had been practicing regularly and during the trials a reporter from the *Manchester Evening News* was most impressed with what he saw. This was probably due to the fact that when he watched the cars racing around the track on their own there was nothing to compare their speed to. The cars, by themselves, looked fast.

The fastest of the Manchester cars were the Farnell Special and the Hulme Special; as the name suggests they were named after their constructors. Frank Farnell was a garage mechanic from the Heaton Moor district of Manchester. Not much is known about the neat little car he created, but one innovation he introduced was a steering wheel cut away at the bottom which gave him more room in the tight cockpit. The other Manchester-built car was assembled by Len Hulme. Hulme's small car was powered by an air-cooled flat twin engine taken from an ABC sports car. ABC had produced small capacity sports cars from 1920 to 27; hence Hulme's engine was at least eight years old. One advantage Hulme's car had over some of the other cars was that over-heating and boiling radiators was eliminated. Having no radiator also saved a fair amount of weight. Hulme had been a frequent visitor to the Belle Vue track as

One of the first genuine Midget Cars to be built in Manchester was Frank Farnel's neat little *Firefly*.

Len Hulme kneels next to a seated Tommy Cooper in his ABC powered Midget.

All the drivers pose for the camera before Belle Vue's first serious Midget Car Meeting.

his motor engineering business was in nearby Ardwick. Unlike Farnell, who was to drive his own car, Hulme engaged one of his own mechanics, Tommy Cooper, to drive. Tommy was from Denton and had been responsible for all the testing that the car had undergone at the track. Both these cars had never turned a wheel in competition unlike the Southern cars which had been gradually developed over the past two years.

The best of the southern cars were the Gillow Specials, a couple of these Brooklands Riley based cars were entered for Victor Gillow and Jimmy Raynes. The majority of the entry consisted of Palmer Specials. Leon Delblat, Raoul Sectarian and Adolf Pabst were engaged to drive these cars. Other interesting cars were Les White's Salmson-engine special and Tommy Sullman's Singer-engine special. Sullman's car sported a radiator taken off a Brescia Bugatti. A car that was always in the headlines was Jean Reville's *Gnat*. This little car was powered by the smallest engine in the line-up, a 500cc speedway JAP. Reville always courted publicity and images of 'the smallest car in the world', appeared in all the leading motoring magazines. Other entries that were published in the *Manchester Evening News* were Frank Varey, once again entered to drive a Gillow Riley, Leon St Nairn, G. Grey, R. (Nobby) Clark and Ginger Norton. One person not mentioned in the *Manchester Evening News* article was Billy Murden. Although never a star Billy always took his own home-built special wherever he might get a drive. Later in the year he and St Nairn even took their cars to Sweden where they gave the first demonstration of Midget Car Racing in Scandinavia. Billy was still racing midget cars as late as 1948!

Although wanting to put on a meeting just for Midget Cars, the management still didn't have enough confidence to do this. Therefore, the first part of the show was for the bikes with the Midgets performing after the interval. Despite the poor weather, and some heavy rain, an estimated crowd of 30,000 crammed themselves into the Hyde Road stadium. Apart from the match races there were to be two main events. The first event consisted of three heats and a final; in each heat there were to be three cars with the first one going forward to the four-car final and the fastest loser making up the fourth place. The concluding event was the big one, with all the cars taking to the track. A couple of the events proved disappointing, as in one heat only two starters came to the line, and in another only three. The heat winners were Murden, DelBlatt and Sulman, and joining these three were Gillow who was the fastest second finisher. In the final Gillow raced into the lead and hugged the inside, Sullman quickly tagged on to his back wheels but was unable to pass. Gillows' winning time was 1 minute 31.2 seconds; a good 3.2 seconds slower than the time Allen Arnold had put up in his Frazer-Nash. The nine-car six-lap race was down to seven starters as two of the cars refused to start. The race turned out to be a duel between local hero Frank Farnell and the more experienced Tommy Sullman as Farnell leapt into the lead with Sullman in hot pursuit. In the wet slippery conditions Farnell over slid on one of the corners letting Sullman through who went on to win in 2 minutes 21 seconds. Farnell finally finished second with DelBlatt third.

Billy Murden's JAP powered car attracted a lot of attention at Sweden's first Midget Car demonstration. (Lars Hageman collection)

Added interest for the local fans had been a match race between the local Hulme special and Reville's little *Gnat*. Instead of the meeting ending on a high, for the Manchester contingent it rather fizzled out. Firstly the ABC engine lived up to its reputation as being rather temperamental. Despite the attention of driver/mechanics Nobby Clark and Tommy Cooper the car refused to start; not a good advert for Len Hulme's garage business. Les White stepped into the breach but in the race the *Gnat*'s motor too faded out, leaving White to come home alone. Compared to the previous car events the majority of fans agreed that it had been a success. A glowing report by 'Broadsider' in the *News Chronicle* stated that, 'Midget motor-car racing on Manchester Belle Vue Speedway track has, in my opinion come to stay'. There were, however, one or two who were not so enthusiastic about the four wheelers. A few disparaging letters were published in the *Belle Vue Bulletin*, mostly from the diehard motorcycle speedway fans.

Another problem to be solved was the attitude of the Motorcycle Speedway Control Board. When the cars were first invited to race on the speedway tracks they banned all their registered riders from taking part in car events. This could have been a serious problem for the Belle Vue management especially as some of their riders wanted to have go at racing Midgets. When Frank Varey drove at the Jubilee meeting this rule didn't affect him as he was supposedly in retirement. The rule banning riders could have caused all sorts of dilemmas; if a rider was determined to drive he could take on an assumed name, as one of Belle Vue's star riders did when he decided to compete in local motorcycle grass track races. Rather than stifle the chance of riders earning a bit of extra cash, a compromise was reached. The Board partially lifted the ban allowing contracted riders to race on their home track but they still weren't allowed to race on other tracks. This sensible decision gave riders a chance to try their hand at car racing and keep abreast of Midget Car development.

Behind the scenes development was going on apace. Regular practice sessions were held on most Wednesdays, but not all sessions went well. A Mr Partington was practicing in his Riley when he lost control, hitting the safety fence and rebounding back across the track onto the centre green. At one of the sessions a driver, who was not wearing a crash helmet, was struck by a stone. The driver was knocked semi-conscious and after losing control he too crashed into the safety fence. The well-tested Hulme special also met with problems, and the troublesome ABC engine was replaced with something a little more reliable. Both a Lancia and a Ford V8 engine were tested. At the practice sessions one person stood out above all the others; Harry Skirrow from Ambleside in the county of Cumberland. Harry already had a certain amount of success racing motorcycles, both on scrambles and speedway. His promising motorcycle career was brought abruptly to an end by a shooting accident in which he lost his left hand. Obviously any aspirations he had had to be a full-time speedway rider were over, but once his left hand had been replaced by a hook he could at least drive a car. Being a regular visitor to Belle Vue speedway he was well aware of the developments that were taking place to introduce Midget Car Racing. He decided he too could build a suitable car; returning to his garage at Ambleside he set about constructing a car that would beat the cars he had seen practicing there. Harry's car was completed in time for the

In 1935 the press were less sensitive about disabilities.

The first Skirrow special was built in just nine days.

July meeting but at the last minute he was taken ill and was unable to attend. Harry and his car had been so outstanding in practice that the Belle Vue management decided to invite him along the following month. In those less politically correct days having only one arm was an advertiser's dream. The *Manchester Evening News* introduced him as, 'The sensational Harry Skirrow, the one armed Lakeland Wonder'. On 24 August, after the Belle Vue v. Hackney Wick speedway match, which Belle lost 30-41, Harry showed his paces. The car performed flawlessly with Harry knocking a whole second off Allen Arnold's four-lap rolling start track record. The record now stood at a very respectable 1 minute 26.1 seconds. Being the last event on the circuit, the track would have been cut up and rough, not at all conducive to fast times. Harry had showed that with a bit more development it wouldn't be long before the cars could achieve similar times to the bikes.

Spotting a worthwhile moneymaking opportunity, Harry decided to cash in on the success of his demonstration. If anyone wanted to purchase a replica of the car then they could do so. A full page advert was placed in the magazine *Speedway News*, offering the car for sale at £150, but we don't know if anyone purchased a replica of the car. Harry had his own ideas as to which way he wanted Midget Car development to go. Back at his Ambleside base he further remodelled his car and came up with a radically new design.

Chapter 4

The US Influence

Spence too had his own agenda so during the closed season he decided to take a trip to the USA. Quite who funded the trip is open to question, but in order to remain in the public eye the Belle Vue theme park needed to constantly update its attractions. What better place to go and check out the very latest developments in entertainment than the United States? Apart from the hottest rides and sideshows Midget Car Racing was the big deal. Spence set sail from Southampton in November aboard the luxury liner *Beringaria*. He first took in some Midget Car Racing in New York before moving on to the mid-west. It was at a Midget Car meeting there that he saw Ronnie Householder racing an Elto. Householder and the Elto were probably the best driver and car combination in the mid-west. Spence was so impressed that after inspecting the car he bought it! The car was loaded on to a trailer and taken back to New York where it was put onto a ship and sent to the UK.

The Elto was one of the best cars around being powered by a two stroke four cylinder out-board motor boat engine. The engine was fitted in a unique way, which was vertically, with the drive shaft pointing down. This engine sat in a chassis built around prefabricated parts taken from Model T Fords.

Purchasing and bringing the car back to the UK was a bold move. He believed he had found just the car for the Belle Vue track. Spence had been away for about four weeks, this gave him approximately five months in which to work out what he wanted to do before the start of 1935. One car was not enough to fill a Midget Car programme so it was decided that copies of the car should be built. Several prospective constructors were available in and around the Manchester area, and Harry Skirrow, Frank Farnell and Len Hulme had all experience in the construction of Midget Cars. With Harry Skirrow hatching out his own plans, Spence had to choose between Farnell and Hulme. He by-passed Farnell and turned to Len Hulme to construct the replicas. He was an ideal choice as he had strong connections with the track and his garage business being regularly advertised in the *Belle Vue Bulletin*. His motor engineering establishment was only a few miles away. Three of his mechanics, Cooper, Warburton and Clark were all well versed in the requirements of midget car building; all three of them having driven the small cars around the Hyde Road Track.

Making several copies of the imported Elto was not as daunting as it might appear. Firstly the Evenrude out board speed boat engine was readily available in the UK. Speed boat racing was quite popular in the north-west; not only was there a hot bed of racing

The H four cylinder two stroke was mounted on end with the crank-shaft pointing in a downwards direction. (Joe Gertlers' Raceway Collection)

in the Lake District but also racing took place on the boating lake in Bell Vue's pleasure gardens. Secondly the running gear, chassis rails, axles etc. were based on pre-fabricated parts taken from the Model T Ford. At one time Model T Fords had been assembled and produced in Manchester at a factory in nearby Trafford Park, so spare parts shouldn't have proved too difficult to source. Once the spare parts were tracked down Hulme and his team began fashioning the chassis. The American ex-midget car racer and motor racing historian Mel Anthony once described how the chassis frames were constructed. He wrote:

> ...the Model T was a major source of steel for most pre-war midgets. They would strip the frame clean off cross members, rivets etc. until they had two rails. The Ford T frame has a slight taper towards the front, and they would use the front half. The right way was to lay out a pattern of tin, cut it to shape for the rear kick-up, then torch the two flanges loose from the web of the Ford channel. Then heat the upper flange, bend it into the desired shape, (with template), and do the same for the lower flange. Now the web remaining in the opening would be discarded, and a piece of Corten steel would be cut to fit the new opening. Corten was a good high carbon steel which matched the Ford T frame material. Now after welding and grinding, the two rails would be fitted with cross members of 'home' manufacture. The front was done the same way by using another template, cutting the flanges loose, and bending the front web into a round type mount for the spring purchase. This time the flanges were discarded, and the web was fitted with new Corton flanges.

The front axles were deliberately made to snap so as to absorb impact if the cars were involved in an accident.

A further tweak that was deemed crucial to the standard parts was the splitting of the front axle. The front axle was cut into two pieces and joined together, again by bolting a piece of metal where the cut had been. The reason for this was that if the front of the car was involved in an accident then the axle would split at its weakest point i.e. the prefabricated joint. This deformable structure would absorb most of the impact thus preventing further expensive damage to the chassis etc. Wheels could have been a problem, but once again the T's parts came to the rescue; the six bolt brake drums from the T were turned down and used as centres for the wheels. To a layman all this may seem rather difficult but to a motor engineer of Hulme's standing it would be a simple process. As was the shaping and forming of the body parts, almost every motor-engineering business of the time had the necessary panel beating hammers, rollers and dollies to mould and form aluminium, or sheet steel, into the desired profiles.

With the car being a proven winner any spare time that would have been spent on development could now be utilised for construction. By the beginning of the 1936 season six cars were up and running but whether they were all new is open to conjecture. Hulme may have constructed just five new ones or the Householder car may have been stripped down copied and rebuilt. Having five or six cars ready was quite an achievement, considering that Hulme had to attend to his motor engineering business as well.

It was all very well having the ideal car but to make midget car racing entertaining decent drivers were needed. More or less anybody could drive a car around a circuit but racing them and acquiring the necessary skills was different matter altogether.

The first six Len Hulme built cars being presented to the public. The drivers are from left to right Bill Kitchen, Acorn Dobson, Eric Worswick, Frank Marsh, Bruce Warburton and Tommy Cooper.

Spence now set about selecting drivers who could do justice to his new car venture. Belle Vue were lucky enough in having a large squad of competent speedway riders, all of whom were used to racing wheel to wheel with no quarter being asked or given. Their top riders were some of the best in the world, if they now fancied their chances at Midget Car racing then the management would now oblige. When the new cars were first introduced to the public in April 1935 two of their speedway riders took part. These were local favourite 'Acorn' Dobson and English international rider Bill Kitchen. Two other cars were driven by Hulme's mechanics, Tommy Cooper and Bruce Warburton. The year before Cooper had helped with the development of the ABC engined Hulme Special and he knew all about throwing a Midget around the Hyde Road track. Warburton also helped with car development, but it was he who had unfortunately crashed the V8 experimental car during testing, badly scalding his legs when the radiator burst. He was fast in the practice sessions and showed tremendous promise with the new Elto. Just being able to afford one of the new Midgets was not enough, Belle Vue wanted drivers who could compete successfully with the other drivers and were able to put up a good show. As it was meant to be a commercial venture, the other two cars were 'customer' cars being sold locally to a couple of drivers who could do the cars justice. One of the 'customer' drivers was Eric Worswick, who at one time had been a member of the speedway squad. The other car now belonged to Frank Marsh; Frank was the proprietor of a well-known garage in leafy Wilmslow.

On the same evening that the Belle Vue Aces were due to race Harringay "Racers" in a speedway league match; the six drivers and cars were presented to the public. The

Postcards of the fans' favourite drivers could be purchased from the supporters' club Kiosk. Here Belle Vue's international speedway star Bill Kitchen poses for his portrait. (Courtesy of Ian Sommerville)

Gorton born Stanley 'Acorn' Dobson. The huge diameter exhaust pipe was a necessary tweak as it helped gases escape and prevented blow back. (Courtesy of Ian Sommerville)

The Boy Wonder Eric Worswick made his Speedway racing debut as a fourteen-year-old at the Salford dirt track. (Courtesy of Clive Worswick)

usual Belle Vue publicity machine swung into action and great things were expected from the new cars. There were now six decent cars all of proven reliability. It was now down to the chosen drivers to produce a good race and put an end all the scepticism that had followed the previous attempts to introduce Midget Car racing. Just one race was planned which went ahead after the Aces had beaten the Racers by 45 points to 31. The win had put the supporters in a very good mood. They were even happier when in the Midget Car race their top rider, Bill Kitchen beat 'Acorn' Dobson by a whisker. All six cars had put on an exciting race their performance impressing the influential journalists. The *News Chronicle* said the race was, '…thoroughly enjoyed…', going on to say that the battle between Dobson and Kitchen was, '…as thrilling a duel as one could witness…'. This national newspaper was so impressed that they even carried a cartoon of the drivers on their sports pages. The drawings making a great play of the smokiness of the two stroke Elto engine. The *Manchester Guardian* also appreciated the cars claiming that, 'They are a great improvement on anything previously tested at Belle Vue'. The journalist also noted the noise of the cars and the spectacle of the, '…sparks and flames spitting from the exhaust'. Spence had landed a winner. Everyone seemed pleased with the initial run; it was now up to the drivers and cars to build on this favourable start.

From that point it was planned to include Midget Cars in every speedway programme. The following week's dramatic advert in the *Manchester Evening News* said, 'More Midget Cars, Small Cars Giving Great thrills taking the bends at Dare Devil Speeds'. This time two races were to take place; a match race between Kitchen

The northern editions of the national daily newspapers took an early interest in Midget Car Racing, sending their reporters to cover events.

and Dobson who had finished first and second the week before, and the second for the other four drivers, with the added novelty of being over six laps. Match races were a great way to test the skills and aggression of the drivers. With only two cars on the track the driver only has to worry about his opponent as there is nobody else cluttering up the track. When trying to overtake around the outside, drivers would know that there wouldn't be anyone else buzzing up on the inside. Similarly if a driver did take a 'blinder' around the fence there wouldn't be any cars in the way. In the match race between Kitchen and Dobson, Kitchen took the lead and Dobson decided to take the long fast line around the outside unfortunately he clattered the fence leaving Kitchen to win his second Midget Car race. In the six-lap race Frank Marsh won in the time of 2 minutes 11.4 seconds.

Over the next three weeks the same six drivers entertained the crowd. Each week a different format was tried; sometimes they raced over six laps at other times four laps. Instead of six cars in a race the maximum was now five; this meant that each week one of the regular drivers stood down. Kitchen, Dobson, Warburton and Worswick competed every week. Cooper missed out the first two weeks; this was probably due to pressure of work; Len Hulme needed to keep the cars in his care in tip top condition. He did turn out on 25 April when he replaced Frank Marsh. The week before Marsh had rather scared himself; his car did a somersault and landed upside down on the track. Fortunately his injuries consisted of nothing more than cuts and bruises. During the thirties there was little concern with driver safety and when an accident happened it was hoped that the driver would be thrown out. If the driver wasn't ejected he could

Frank Marsh was one of the first drivers to recognise the need for driver safety. (Courtesy of Harry Marsh)

get injured under the car and after his accident Frank fitted a rather crude roll over bar; thus if he once again found himself upside-down this new device would protect him. At the time it was said that unless he fitted the roll bar his mother would have stopped him from racing! When Frank realised that the extra weight of the roll bar was holding him back he quickly jettisoned it, preferring to face the wrath of his mother rather than remain uncompetitive.

Six weeks into the season, other drivers started to come forward, some more serious than others. With the Pleasure Gardens playing host to many entertainers and sportsmen it was no surprise that some of them would like to have a go at driving one of the Midget Cars. When Jock McAvoy, a British and Commonwealth Light-Heavyweight boxing champion, was taking part in a championship bout in Belle Vue's Kings Hall, he was persuaded to try out a Midget Car. This second-rate publicity stunt generated not only exposure for his forthcoming fight but gained extra press coverage for the cars. One of the more serious trainees was Fred Alexander who had performed so well in trials that for the last meeting in May a car was prepared for him. With Marsh out injured and Kitchen and Dobson taking a break from the cars the other drivers in the race were Worswick, Warburton and Cooper. All three of them were by now fairly experienced racers and their track craft shone through in the race. Worswick won in a time of 1 minute 24.8 seconds, which equalled the track record he had set the week before. Fred's immaturity showed up in the race when he came last; which proved that racing around the track on his own was one thing, but mastering the rolling start and having drivers in close proximity was another.

Taking every opportunity to maximise their profits Belle Vue put on extra meetings for the Bank Holidays. Whit Monday was to be no exception. As the drivers were now getting to grips with their cars times were beginning to tumble; Worswick was now putting in some decent times. At the Whit Monday meeting he knocked a further 1.2 seconds off his four lap rolling start track record; the Midgets were now getting closer to their goal, which was to be as fast as the bikes. At the moment they were about three or four seconds slower. On that same bank holiday there was another Midget Car race taking place a few miles west along the East Lancashire Road. Ominously this race was to shake up Midget Car racing in Manchester and was between Harry Skirrow and Walter Mackereth. When Spence decided to hand over the development of the Elto Midgets to Len Hulme it left Skirrow rather out in the cold. This meant that when it came to track testing time Hulme's cars had priority over Skirrow's. Perhaps in a fit of pique Skirrow did a deal with Liverpool speedway and took his cars to that city's Stanley Stadium.

All sorts of shows visited the Pleasure Gardens, one of the famous ones being the 'wall of death' motorcyclists. The stadium also put on the occasional shows from the Armies' motorcycle display teams to individual trick motorcyclists and stunt riders. Probably the finest stunt troupe to visit the stadium was Putt Mossman's 'Rodeo Motorcycle Circus'. This famous American group travelled the world with a company of professional performers. Not only was Putt Mossman a brilliant stunt man, he was

Legendry stunt man Putt Mossman was a match for many a professional motorcycle Speedway rider.

also an accomplished motorcycle speedway rider and Midget Car driver. On Saturday 6 June Mossman paid a visit to Manchester, after the speedway meeting he gave a brief demonstration of stunt riding. Seeing the Midget Cars in the pits it was no surprise that Putt took the gamble to race against the local stars. He lined up against Worswick, Warburton and the rapidly improving Alexander. But before that race Putt's sister Dessie, who was part of the travelling show, went out to show that women too could handle a Midget Car. The speedway fraternity was not yet ready for women to race against the men. Just racing around on her own would have been a pointless exercise; to make her run more noteworthy the exhibition was to be over three laps. This old ploy allowed a new record to be established. Dessie impressed everyone with her smooth and fast run; she set up a very creditable time of 1 minute 3.6 seconds, which compared favourably with the four-lap record. In the main Midget Car race Putt gave the Mancunians a lesson in showmanship and taught them how close racing should be. He stole a march at the start and kept Bruce Warburton behind him by using every part of the track. Every time Bruce closed up on him Putt blocked the move and the crowd loved the duel, even though his time was only 1 minute 27.6 seconds which was four seconds slower than Eric Worswick's best time.

Midget Cars were now a recognised part of speedway's Saturday night's entertainment. Instead of following a set formula, each weekend a different type of race was staged. There was a match race between a now fully recovered Frank Marsh and Eric Worswick, which Worswick won. Dessie Mossman's three lap record was lowered to 1 minute 3.4 seconds by Bruce Warburton; Bruce knocking only 0.2 of a second from her time, which emphasised what a polished performer Dessie was. The press were warming to the Midgets claiming that before the end of the season the cars would match the times of the bikes. This was no idle talk from the media, especially as newcomer Fred Alexander had sensationally lowered the four lap track record to 1 minute 23.6 seconds. Fred managed to set this time in the first heat of a two heats and final type event. In the final Alexander was unable to follow this up; he finished third behind Worswick and Dobson.

If Belle Vue wished Midget Car Racing was to stand on its own then more cars and drivers were needed. This was something Spence knew when he first commissioned the building of the first batch of cars. Now that the public and press were taking a greater interest, Spence and Hulme embarked on their second phase. A new batch of specials were about to be fabricated. This time they were to be offered to the public; but there were certain conditions. Not just anybody could buy one; they were to go only to approved applicants. No doubt Hulme could have easily sold this second batch, after all he was the only person in Greater Manchester offering Midget Cars for sale. At the beginning of July an advert was placed in the *Belle Vue Bulletin* offering 'Genuine American Type Midgets' for sale at the price of £195. Before the advert was placed in the programme Hulme must have had a couple of cars ready, because within a week of the advertisement appearing eight cars were entered for the Midget Car races.

Now that there were eight cars available it was possible to have two four-car heats and a final. This well used format, with the first and second going through to the final, was the mainstay of many a second-half motorcycle speedway meeting. A new name

£195 FOR SALE £195

TO APPROVED APPLICANTS

Genuine American Type Midgets

For full particulars apply to :
THE MANAGER,
BELLE VUE SPEEDWAY,
MANCHESTER, 12

Len Hulme was now ready to take orders for the second batch of his 'American Midgets'.

appeared in the list of competitors, that of Arthur Marcos, who was to make his debut in the second heat. Like all novices he was out to make an impression; he tore past Alexander, missed the next corner and almost turned back into him! His wayward driving upset one or two of the fans, who ought not to have been too harsh on him as the track was rather damp, conditions Arthur may not have encountered before. For the final the track must have been in very poor state, because the winner, Frank Marsh, could only manage a time of 1 minute 32.4 seconds and star driver Bill Kitchen never made the final.

Once again over the next two weeks the formula for the Midgets was shuffled around. Worswick won a five-car race over six laps and Fred Alexander beat Frank Marsh in a match race. Over the August Bank Holiday weekend there was to be a meeting on Saturday and an extra meeting on Monday. The twist for the Manchester Midget Car fans was that two new drivers and cars were booked to appear at the Saturday night meeting. These two drivers were to show the Manchester chaps how Midget Car Racing should be were Walter Mackereth and the one-armed wonder himself Harry Skirrow. During the past year Harry had put his fertile mind into remodelling what he thought the perfect Midget should be. With no purpose-built track near his home base of Ambleside he looked around for a suitable venue. Within easy driving distance was

After much testing the very latest four-wheel drive Skirrow was launched on the Market.

the vast expanse of Morecambe Bay with a huge stretch of open flat hard sand. It was at Flookburgh on the north side of the Bay that Harry and his team of mechanics tried out different ideas. They tried front-wheel drive and rear-wheel drive, but the set up they were most excited about was four-wheel drive. It was this radically designed car that Mackereth and Skirrow were to show off that Bank Holiday. Chassis design and drive chain wouldn't be much use without a decent engine; in the thirties there were several proprietary engines to choose from. The engine that Harry chose was the 8/80 V-Twin JAP. Quite how this particular engine was conceived is open to conjecture; basically it was based on two 500cc air-cooled speedway engines set at 50 degrees on a common crankcase. It is claimed that it was Skirrow himself who persuaded JAP to build this engine and that such an engine could be a profitable proposition. JAP listened to Skirrow and had the engine in full production by the end of 1936. So confident was JAP of their engines' suitability for Midget Car racing that by the end of the year they were exporting them to the USA the home of Midget Car racing.

Everybody at the track was anxious to see how the new cars would perform. Rather than pitch them in straight away against the Eltos, a match race between Skirrow and Mackereth preceded the main Midget Car Races. The cars went well, Mackereth leading home his boss Harry Skirrow. In the main event, the first heat was won by 'Acorn' Dobson but it was the second heat that ended any complacency the local drivers may have had when Walter Mackereth vanished into the distance. Joining Mackereth and

MIDGET J-A-P MOTOR

Here is the engine you have been waiting for—a twin cylinder, overhead valve unit, especially developed for midget car racing.

80 B.H.P. at 6000 R.P.M.

Ball and roller bearing throughout—separate carburetors—weight only 122 pounds complete. Send for complete specifications and performance figures.

RACING HEADQUARTERS

Approved Crash Helmets $9.50
John Bull Midget Tires .. 4.90
Unbreakable Mask Goggles
$2.50 and up

Exclusive United States Distributors

PINK · VOICHICK

Inc.

Southern Boulevard
at E. 180th St., Bronx, New York

At the end of 1936 the 8/80 V-twin JAP was being offered for sale in the United States.

Dobson in the final were Warburton and Harry himself. Again Walter streaked away leaving the Eltos to struggle in his wake.

Two days later it was Bank Holiday Monday and this time there were no outsiders involved. All eight local cars and drivers raced in just two heats, there was to be no final. Fred Alexander won the first race and Bruce Warburton the second, neither driver matching the times that Mackereth had achieved on the Saturday.

The day after the bank holiday turned out to be a rather disputatious date in UK Midget Car history. On Tuesday 4 August at Hackney Wick stadium London the World Midget Car Championship was held! This was a rather grandiose title for an individual event. Only nine drivers took part; with only three cars per race. The most important thing that can be said about the meeting was that it showcased the Skirrow Special. Quite how it could be described as a championship of any kind was rather ludicrous; it was a great injustice to the Manchester drivers as none of them were invited along. The Skirrows dominated the event which was won by US motorcycle speedway star Cordy Milne. Two other Americans took part in the event, stunt artistes Putt Mossman and Bob Deihl. Incidentally Bob was a member of Mossman's troupe. So fascinated was Mossman with the Skirrow that he purchased one of them and added it to his stable of bikes.

Belle Vue Stadium was available throughout the week; accordingly the management were able to put on whatever event they wished. Being dedicated to entertainment and showmanship they allowed Putt Mossman to bring along the full complement of his Motorcycle Rodeo Circus. Putt thrilled the crowd with his usual accomplished stunt

One of the first customers for the Skirrow Special was Putt Mossman who added one of the four-wheel drive cars to his stunt show.

performances. But he and his team couldn't resist the chance to show off their new midget car. In a match race against Eric Worswick he stunned the local midget car fraternity by knocking TWO whole seconds off the track record; leaving it at 1 minute 21.4 seconds. His compatriot, Bob Deihl was not so effective and could only finish third behind 'Acorn' Dobson and Arthur Marcus.

After the Mossman show it should have been back to normal; the main motorcycle speedway meeting followed by the Midget Car races. This being England it was inevitable that at some time during the summer rain would intervene. Predictably rain fell during the Belle Vue verses Wembley speedway match, causing the rest of the meeting to be abandoned, including the Midgets. Racing did return the following week with a match race between the ever improving Arthur Marcus and 'Acorn' Dobson; the *News Chronicle* readily reporting, '...midget cars continue to improve with every meeting...'. Dobson's winning time a splendid 1 minute 23.8 seconds.

Now that there were more cars available a new name appeared on the scene. This newcomer was to become one of the legends of Midget Car racing at Belle Vue. Charlie Pashley, or as everyone called him, 'Ginger', was no stranger to the oval scene in Manchester. He had raced bikes on all sorts of tracks; from the very first dirt track at Audenshaw to the sands of Southport. His Midget Car debut at Belle Vue was a baptism of fire. In his first competitive race he was thrown in with seven other drivers and this number of cars all flat out and diving into the first turn could, and more often than not, spell trouble. Sure enough, Arthur Marcus was the unlucky one; he crashed, and as a result suffered cuts and bruising. Charlie kept out of trouble but was not in the first three, Eric Worswick won in 1 minute 24 seconds followed by Fred Alexander and Frank Marsh. The other drivers were Warburton, Cooper and Dobson.

There were now seven out and out Midget car racers in Manchester, all of them dedicated to making to the cars a success. Apart from these northerners there were

When the Midget Car team became established Charlie Pashley was the natural choice as team captain. (Rod Pashley collection)

others who could see the marketable potential of the Midgets. From the first time that Harry Skirrow saw the Midgets he knew there was an opening for this new form of motor racing. Being a regular visitor to Belle Vue he met up with other parties who were intent on making money out of Midgets. One of those showing an interest was Jimmy Baxter, an experienced Speedway promoter who had been involved in speedway promotion ever since it first came to this country. Baxter and Skirrow formed a partnership to exploit the situation; Baxter had the entrepreneurial flair and Skirrow the practical engineering skills. The two of them went ahead with their plans deciding that Holland was just the place to test out their schemes and theories! On the day after the eight car race at Manchester several Southern based cars and drivers took their Midgets to race at the Woudenstein dirt track near Rotterdam. Because of the clashing dates none of the regular Belle Vue drivers made the trip to Holland. Nevertheless one Manchester driver who did make the journey was Frank Farnell. Ever since Spence favoured Len Hulme with the construction of the Eltos, Farnell had been out in the cold. He leapt at the chance to take his car, the *Firefly* over to the Netherlands. Frank didn't finish among the winners, which was only to be expected as he was up against the very latest Skirrows. The meeting was won by the rising star of Midget Car Racing Walter Mackereth. All Frank could manage was a second place behind Jimmy Raynes in heat 6.

In Manchester the 1936 season was drawing to a close; the Midget drivers made the most of the last few weeks of the season. They appeared on the programme with a full complement of drivers at every meeting. During these last few meetings not one driver dominated the results; honours being shared evenly. Worswick won a five-car race on 26 September, Arthur Marcus won the final of the two heats and a final event the following week. The highlight of the season was the racing that happened on 10 October, when no less than ten cars and drivers were available. Marcus, Worswick, Dobson, Kitchen and Marsh lined up in the first race. Alexander, Pashley, Warburton, Cooper and Nobby Clarke were in the second. The lucky ones who made it to the final

Above: Bob Deihl (No 8) was a star performer in the Putt Mossman stunt shows, a few weeks earlier he had competed at Hackney Wicks world championship meeting. Here he takes the outside line at the Woudestein meeting. (Paul Hooft collection)

Left: Denton's Tommy Cooper gets the Elto sideways.

were Worswick, Cooper, Marcus and rapidly emerging Pashley. Pashley finished a very respectable third behind Worswick and Cooper.

With plenty of cars available for the last meeting of season; there were to be no less than four races. The very last race of the night was a grand finale with eight cars all vying to be the last winner of 1936. A couple of heats and a final were planned and at the last minute the grand finale had been added to the programme; this was no doubt due to the carnival atmosphere surrounding the end of term high-jinx. A very busy Bill Kitchen won the final, beating Worswick, Dobson and Pashley. Just before the first Midget Car heat Bill had climbed off his speedway bike and jumped straight into a midget car; and this after he had finished second behind Aussie great Max Grosskreutz in what was the last motorcycle speedway race of the year. Rather than risk all ten cars in the grand finale only eight came to the line, the unfortunate two who missed out were Frank Marsh and Bruce Warburton. Keeping up the tradition of the previous weeks it was Tommy Cooper's turn to cross the line first.

The 1936 season was now over. Midget Car Racing hadn't exactly swept the country in the same way as the bikes had earlier in the decade. This had been the third year of car racing at Belle Vue and some headway had been made. Decent cars were now available, but above all the drivers now knew how to drive fast and competitively. To a certain degree Spence had achieved what he had set out to do; rather than rush ahead and put on sub-standard Midget Car Racing he had taken his time making sure that when the time came professional, well run, close exciting racing would be seen by the Manchester public. In certain quarters it was felt that the time was right for Midget Car Racing to stand on its own two feet. During the closed season plans were being made to bring this about. In the London area several tracks had been staging full Midget Car programmes ever since 1934. Even after three years the necessary breakthrough had not yet taken place; probably due to the fact that the cars had not been up to the standard required. The following year all of this was to change dramatically.

Chapter 5

The Optimistic Year

On the few occasions that Harry Skirrow had turned up at Belle Vue his cars had dominated the racing. If he wished to expand his interest in cars he had to look further afield as the door for further expansion at Belle Vue seemed to be firmly shut. After their continental experiment Harry Skirrow and Jimmy Baxter took the bull by the horns and set up a company to promote Midget Car Racing in the UK. The company (Car Speedways Ltd) negotiated with the owners of the Lea Bridge and Coventry stadiums to run full midget car speedway meetings. Both of them had been former motorcycle speedway tracks, Coventry's last bike meeting taking place there in 1936. Lea Bridge on the other hand had been running Midget Car Races since 1934. Baxter and Skirrow tidied up both tracks and intended to operate them in the same professional way that motorcycle speedway meetings were organised. No longer was Midget Car Racing to be conducted by well-meaning clubs run by amateurs. One further step that was taken was the setting up of a body of officials who could supervise the running of meetings. Whether it was London or Manchester the same set of rules and regulations would apply. Baxter, Skirrow and one or two others, Spence included, had changed the whole set up of Midget Car Racing; it was now on a sound commercial footing whose sole purpose was to make money, which after all was what Spence was hoping to do with his initial involvement with Midgets. To be closer to the action in London and Coventry, Skirrow moved his whole car-making operation to Tottenham. It was here that he rented workshops from Victor Martin. Martin not only made motorcycle speedway bikes but also had close connections with J. A. Prestwich the manufacturer of the 8/80 JAP that was used in Skirrows' cars. As yet Car Speedways didn't have enough cars and drivers of their own to stage meaningful meetings. This dearth of competitive cars meant that if they were prepared to travel, the Manchester drivers could race their cars at other venues. In the south there were several home-built specials that Car Speedways could call upon but what they really wanted were cars of their own. During the winter Skirrows' small group of mechanics worked flat out to have sufficient cars ready for 1937.

Prospects for the 1937 season were looking very rosy. In Manchester it began on 27 March with just one race for six cars, which was won by Eric Worswick. The line-up was a little different from the previous year as Frank Farnell made a very rare appearance. As it was the Easter weekend, an extra Speedway meeting was held on

Bank Holiday Monday. The one Midget Car Race was notable as it was won by Charlie Pashley. Charlie, or 'Ginger' as he was better known by his fans, had adapted to Midget Cars particularly well. He was now a match for any of the local drivers as this first win had illustrated. Throughout the month of April provision was made for a Midget Car Race to be held after every speedway fixture. With just one race per meeting it was an undemanding way to ease the drivers into what would turn out be a hectic season.

In other parts of the country Midget Car racing was about to take off. Coventry opened for business on 2 May; the following week Glasgow put on their first meeting. The Glasgow opener was a stirring Scotland versus England international match. Back in Manchester, and throughout the early part of May, the format remained the same, with just one race after the main event. The third Saturday in May saw a complete change in the lifestyle and fortunes of the Manchester-based drivers. First and foremost the Hyde Road Stadium was reserved for motorcycle speedway racing; the bikes took precedent over all other forms of entertainment. It was because of this set up that the drivers were restricted to the odd race after the main event. With the opening of Coventry, Glasgow and Lea Bridge an opportunity now arose which would make Midget Cars the major attraction. To fill the line-ups, cars and drivers were in huge demand and the Manchester drivers now had to adapt a more professional approach. They had been used to one meeting a week, with at the most two races, but now with extra bookings flooding in cars and drivers had to be prepared to race five or six times a meeting. Not only were there more races per meeting but they could also be competing two or three times a week. More meetings meant more preparation; the cars needed cleaning and polishing, tyres changed, engines checked and tuned. A great deal of additional work and planning were needed, and other factors also had to be taken into account. It was one thing to transport their cars the few short miles from around the suburbs of Manchester, but another to tow them to London, Glasgow and all the tracks in-between. Large reliable cars and dependable trailers were needed.

The Manchester drivers' first away engagement proved to be an anti-climax. Four of them, Worswick, Warburton, Marsh and Pashley agreed to accept a booking to take their cars along to Coventry's second meeting. Unfortunately the British weather put paid to this, as heavy rain forced the meeting to be abandoned. Their disappointment was somewhat tempered when they were invited back the following week. For the first time in quite a while Hyde Road was not to see the Midgets do battle after the bikes had done their bit. Instead the Manchester drivers were to experience their first taste of team racing. They had been invited by the promoters of Glasgow to bring along a team to the White City Stadium, Ibrox. Here they were to represent Manchester in an inter-city challenge match against a team representing Glasgow. And what an experience this first team match turned out to be! Pashley, Marsh, Worswick and Cooper made the trip to Scotland. Two drivers from each city were to race over six heats, and the scoring was a little different from the usual speedway formula. Instead of three points for win it was two points for a win; second gained one point which meant that those drivers finishing third and fourth didn't record any points. The Glasgow drivers all drove the latest four-wheel drive Skirrows. These cars were all owned by the Glasgow promoters who loaned them to the Scottish drivers. None of the Scots had had much

One of the Glasgow team's Skirrow just manages to escape smashing into one of the centre green flag poles. (John Hyam collection)

experience of racing and, as can be imagined, this lack of experience showed. There were crashes galore. *The Bulletin*, a Glasgow newspaper of the period, reported that, 'Time after time the stretcher-bearers waiting at the bends for causalities jumped to attention when first one driver and then another crashed through the fence.' In the first race Murry Frame (Glasgow), Pashley and Marsh had all become entangled with the wire fence. In a later race Eric Worswick, Jim Feeley (Glasgow) and Fag Wilson (Glasgow) all ended up on the greyhound track. In the end Glasgow won by 12 points to 6; with Charlie Pashley being the only driver to win a race for Manchester. During and after the match tempers flared and the usual Scottish partisan crowd took every opportunity they had to denigrate the English! The bad feeling that was floating around the stadium was exacerbated by the crowd's behaviour. When the Manchester drivers returned home they claimed that the Glaswegian drivers were more interested in knocking them off the track rather than winning the races. After the meeting a hostile crowd gathered around the Mancunians and seemed intent on driving them out of town. Charlie Pashley took matters into his own hands and with a well-placed blow hit one of the protesters with his empty two gallon fuel can. This can with the perfect indentation of a head resided in the Pashley workshop for several years as a reminder of never to return to Glasgow!

After the excitement of their first taste of racing on another track; it was back to Manchester for just one race on Saturday night after the speedway meeting; a race won by Charlie Pashley from Eric Worswick. The following day, Sunday 23 May, it was up early, sort out the cars from the previous night's racing, and then make their way to Coventry's Brandon Stadium. Rather than taking on Harry Skirrow's cars straight away they were given the opportunity to race against one another after which there was to be a series of match races. This gave them the opportunity to get the feel of the track before taking on Car Speedway's regular drivers. This turned out to be another culture shock for the Manchester drivers. The four of them opened the programme with a rolling start four lap race; their performance didn't exactly endear them with the Coventry fans. The temperamental two-stroke Elto's spluttered around for their two warm up laps and then refused to behave when the starter dropped the flag. Only Charlie Pashley managed to coax his engine into life and was the only finisher; not a very good start for the Northerners. Consequently their proposed attempts on the track record were thankfully cancelled. Some credit was redeemed when Eric Worswick and Frank Marsh won their match races against Syd Emery and Stan Mills respectively. Charlie Pashley was less fortunate in his match race; the flying Walter Mackereth taking the honours. The most interesting feature of this meeting was the main event which was a team event between a squad representing London and a team dubbed the Provinces. Team racing was the ultimate goal of those now running Midget Car racing. Having seen how successful this form of racing was within the motorcycle speedway community the Midget Car promoters wanted the same arrangement for their sport. But all that would have to wait until enough cars were built and drivers trained up.

The appearance of the Belle Vue drivers in London made the headlines in the speedway press.

On the Wednesday after the Coventry calamity another new experience was in store. The 'Four Manchester Lads' had been requested to appear at London's Lea Bridge track. This was the second meeting at the newly revamped track. Since 1934 Lea Bridge had seen several different people trying to establish midget car racing around the former (Leyton) Orient football ground. A dramatic change in the stadium's fortunes took place when Harry Skirrow and Jimmy Baxter's Car Speedways Company took over the lease to run midgets; it was now to be run as a purely money making concern. Their two tracks at Coventry and Lea Bridge could now offer regular racing for interested parties. One great advantage these two tracks had over other Midget Car venues was that they didn't have to share their facilities with the motorcycle speedway fraternity. They could operate on a weekly basis and have none of the problems associated with the track preparation that the bikes demanded. When the Manchester Lads arrived at London they found that the Lea Bridge programme was exactly the same as Coventry's Sunday meeting i.e. their own race followed by other races. The main feature event was team racing between London and The Provinces. None of the Northern drivers turned out for either of these two teams; no doubt it was felt that they needed more knowledge of away tracks before tacking on the Southern drivers.

In the past few days our Manchester heroes had raced at three different tracks in five days! Cars needed servicing and drivers needed a break from travelling up and down the country. Not only were they racing on week nights and weekends but they were also in full time employment and having to hold down jobs. A few days away from racing was a welcome break. Even though the Midgets were still taking a break from the Belle Vue track; those who wished could still find plenty of racing with the Car Speedways set up.

By the beginning of June the idea of setting up team racing, with regular and established teams, was being mooted. Car Speedways approached the Manchester drivers to see if they would be part of a team that would represent their city for a couple of meetings against Coventry and Lea Bridge. There was one big problem with this, not all Belle Vue based Midget Car drivers were willing to take time out and travel to away venues. At the end of 1936 there had been several decent drivers around, for one reason or another not all of them had continued with their Midget Car career. Bill Kitchen and 'Acorn' Dobson were contracted speedway riders and as such were unavailable. Arthur Marcus had disappeared from the Belle Vue scene, as had Fred Alexander. Fred though had not exactly given up Midget Car racing as he had decamped to Norwich where he gave several displays against other drivers. Other former drivers had just drifted away.

The dates set aside for a team event were 6 June at Coventry and 9 June at Lea Bridge. The Manchester squad was the usual four plus a couple of the Northwest drivers who had been competing on the Car Speedway's tracks. The two new Manchester team members were Syd Plevin and Joe Wildblood. Syd was from Ormskirk and had previously raced bikes at Belle Vue. When he first began racing bikes a great future had been predicted, but he was never quite able to fulfil that early promise. Joe was still in the novice stage, this being his first season with the cars. Joe had regularly attended Belle Vue making the forty- mile trip from his hometown of Rock Ferry on the Wirral via the newly-opened Mersey Tunnel. Both Syd and Joe had their first taste of Midget

A great motorcycle speedway future was predicted for Syd Plevin before he transferred to Midget Car Racing.

Joe was still racing Skirrows twenty-three years later in 1960 when he appeared in a Midget Car meeting in Holland. (Courtesy of Doug Wildblood)

Car racing at Liverpool when Harry Skirrow's outfit was domiciled there, so it was no surprise that the pair of them were driving the latest Skirrow's.

Both contests were over nine heats; with six drivers representing their respective teams. The usual scoring system being used was three points for a win, two for second and one for third. At Coventry the Manchester drivers put up a rather lacklustre performance they suffered from far too many mechanical problems. Consequently they lost 32 points to 20. The highest scorer was team captain Charlie Pashley and the only visitor to win a race was Syd Plevin. A feature of the main event was that all the team races were rolling starts. This was necessary as the Eltos weren't fitted with clutches. This rather irked the Coventry fans who were used to standing starts. Races there were usually started by an electronic starting gate and not at the drop of a flag as was the norm at contemporary motor race meetings. The following week several irate letters were published in the Coventry programme complaining about the poor performance of the Eltos. One scribe penned a poem about the Midgets which contained the verse

> And oh dear those 'Eltos' three
> Make a noise just like a bee
> Alas, Alas, what's Pashley doing
> If he's not careful we'll all be booing.

Basil deMattos continued his racing car career well into the forties and fifties driving a F2 Cromard in several major UK Motor Race meetings.

Three days later the lads travelled to Lea Bridge. It was more or less the same set of drivers except that, because of business commitments, Joe Wildblood was replaced by Basil deMattos. Basil was based at Lea Bridge so his inclusion in the team should have helped the cause. Because there were more than enough drivers based at Lea Bridge, Jimmy Raynes was included as reserve. Even with the boost in numbers the team fared no better; after nine heats they went down again, this time losing by 34 points to 20. Charlie Pashley tried desperately hard for his team, managing to win two races.

The rest of June saw many changes in the direction of those involved with Midget Car Racing at Belle Vue. Firstly the principal promoters connected with the Midget Car scene decided to organise 'proper' team racing which had been their goal all along. It was team racing that had been the saviour of motorcycle speedway racing. Once the initial euphoria of seeing individual riders vying for separate honours had worn off a new direction was needed. To make meetings a little more attractive team racing was tagged on to the end of the main events. These became so popular that they began to dominate the procedings; which in turn led to the formation of a National League. One of the prime movers behind the creation of league racing was Jimmy Baxter, who at the time was a prominent motorcycle speedway promoter. Now that Baxter had switched to cars he wished to apply his expertise to Midget Car Racing, which in his eyes meant team racing. At the time only two tracks were fully committed to Midgets which were the Car Speedway's tracks. To introduce team racing on a league basis Car Speedways needed to be creative. With enough capable drivers around they could put together four six man teams. It was decided that Provinces and Coventry could be based at Brandon; and that Lea Bridge and London could use the Lea Bridge facilities. Once the league was up and running it was assumed that other speedway tracks could join in. A four team league meant that any late comers could easily participate. Several motorcycle speedway tracks had been running Midget Cars after their main presentations. Wembley, Harringay, West Ham, Southampton and several others had all given the cars a try. Any one of them could have put together a team to swell the league. Rather than join in straightaway the promoters held back, no doubt waiting to see how profitable the new venture would be. Baxter and Skirrow contacted Spence to see if he was interested in joining up. Belle Vue could quite easily accommodate Midget Car meetings as the stadium was available on any weekday. The bikes traditionally raced on Saturday nights. Spence though declined as he had something rather spectacular up his sleeve. With no team to represent Manchester it meant that the northern drivers could join up with the newly created teams.

The thrilling event that Spence was about to unleash on the public was scheduled for 26 June. On that day the Belle Vue 'Aces' speedway team were racing away at Harringay, which meant that there was a spare date. On that day Spence planned to showcase the Midgets with a real spectacular display. With Belle Vue being Belle Vue they really pushed the boat out for this extra special meeting. With the backing of the other midget car promoters they were to hold The Speedway Car Championship of Great Britain with a prize fund being advertised at a staggering £500!!! This was a phenomenal amount of money; especially when one considers that a new three bedroomed semi-detached house in upmarket Wilmslow could be bought for £395. How the figure of

A full night's entertainment was guaranteed for the Speedway Car Championship of Great Britain.

£500 was arrived at is a mystery and it is doubtful if much of this money would have found its way into the driver's pockets. The *Midland Daily Telegraph* gives a hint as to how the prize fund was shared out; when they wrote, '…a purse of £60 has been put up for the winner…' a rather small percentage of the advertised £500. Big prize money was nothing new on the dirt tracks. In the late twenties and throughout the thirties motorcycle speedway riders were the highest paid sportsmen of the time. In later years Frank Varey recalled that, '…it was the speedway riders and not the footballers who were driving the flash cars…' A further example of their earning power was given by Jack Ormston. His obituary in the *Daily Telegraph* of 26 June 2007 claimed that he would get £100 appearance money at provincial meetings plus any prize money. It was said that he would expect to earn £15,000 in a season.

Sixteen of the best Midget Car drivers in the county were invited along. Strangely for an individual event they were to race over sixteen heats compared to the classic twenty heat individual formula. Seven of the participants were aboard the JAP powered four-wheel drive Skirrows. Les White brought along his well sorted Salmson powered special. Two cars that had been constructed by Australian Tommy Sullman were also entered, one for Sullman himself, who was to drive his Singer powered car, the other for Jimmy Raynes. Raynes's car was powered by an Anzani engine and the rest of the field was made up by the locally built Eltos.

Now that the Manchester drivers were competing against other types of cars it was becoming obvious that their cars were being left behind. Nothing demonstrated this

After the war Tommy Sullman had the Sullman Singer flown to Australia, where it remains to this day. (Ivan Dutton collection)

Jimmy Raynes was to remain in the Motor Racing industry. When Laystall Engineering produced a Grand Prix car in the early fifties they turned to him to reconstruct the rear suspension. (Ivan Dutton Collection)

Charlie Pashley admires the ease in which the V-twin JAP slotted into the Eltos chassis. (Rod Pashley Collection)

more than the poor performance that the cars had put up in the two team matches against Coventry and Lea Bridge. The cars' inferior performances were further underlined at Coventry on 20 June when Eric Worswick and Charlie Pashley finished a very poor last in a best pairs' event. It was nothing to do with driver ability as both of them were fast and competent. To remain competitive the Eltos needed some serious development. The chassis that Len Hulme had built had proved to be well handling, strong and reliable; it was the power unit that was the Achilles heel. Hulme had tried fitting different power units none of which proved suitable; mainly because he had used water cooled engines. Good as these units were, he was never able to solve over-heating problems. To improve their cars the Belle Vue management took the wise decision to hand over car development to Charlie Pashley. Charlie realised that the Two Stroke Evenrude engine was no match for the 8/80 v-twin JAP. To compete on equal terms the JAP engine needed to be shoehorned into the Elto chassis. A new 8/80 JAP was ordered and it was hoped that it could be fitted to his car in time for the big championship event. The engine was delivered at twelve noon on the day of the championship! Charlie and his helpers worked all through the afternoon to fit the new engine. Being skilled motor engineers they would no doubt have had the old engine out and new engine plates prefabricated, fitted and lined up ready to take the JAP. All the mechanics' work paid off and by the time the first race was due to start Charlie was ready to go taking his place alongside the other racers.

With Belle Vue's usual flair the meeting went off well and the maintenance staff had prepared the track perfectly. The headlines in the following week's *Speedway World* bore this out with a headline that read 'Putt Mossman's Record Smashed by Spike Rhiando by 3 secs'. It was in the first heat, when the track was at its best, that Spike left the track record at a magnificent 78.4 seconds. The speed of the cars was now within touching distance of the bikes' track record. Now that the car times were similar to those of the bikes' times they were reported in seconds rather than minutes and seconds. This might seem a trivial point but psychologically it meant that the cars and the bikes were now on an equal footing. The big prize money and the prestige of being British Champion was a huge incentive with every driver wanting to shine. The destination of the championship can be said to have been decided in the second and sixth heat. In the second heat Walter Mackereth and Vic Patterson raced into the lead, the pair of them side by side until Walter overdid it on one of the bends. This caused him to slide wide and let Vic through to score his first victory. A very popular winner of heat three was Harry Skirrow, and the crowd appreciated his one arm driving skills. In the next heat there was an even more popular winner. Charlie Pashley delighted the home audience with the recently altered Elto coming home first. In the sixth heat Tommy Sullman had the daunting task of taking on Rhiando, Patterson and Skirrow, all of them unbeaten. With all three of them determined to remain in the chase for the championship, something was bound to give. Rhiando and Skirrow were dicing wheel to wheel whenSkirrow over-slid. Unable to correct the slide he hit Rhiando's car with force. This broke the drop arm, which caused the car to collide with the fence, and put Spike out of the running. Patterson was right behind the both of them and missed Spike by inches. Skirrow now found himself in the lead; but he over-cooked it on one of the bends and he too thumped the fence letting Patterson through to win his second race. Sullman benefited from the accidents and came home second. The rest of the heats passed off without incident, except perhaps heat seven when Stan Mills took a spectacular charge around the outside. Coming out of a turn he was closing fast on two drivers in front of him. Unable to lift off in time he collided with one of them. This broke his axle which caused his retirement from the race. The winner of the championship was in doubt right up until the final race. Pashley's new JAP powered Elto had performed fantastically; three wins and one second left him sitting on eleven points. Mackereth too had the same score. Patterson had three wins under his belt from three races. To make certain of the championship Vic had to win; second place would see a three-way tie between Pashley, Mackereth and Patterson, third or fourth was not an option. This last heat decider was a promoter's dream and all eyes were on Vic. More drama was created when George Turvey came out for this last race driving Walter Mackereth's car. All sorts of conspiracy theories could have been written into this. Mackereth needed Turvey to finish in front of Patterson. If Turvey could do this then Mackereth would be in the run off. In a run off situation Walter would be the clear favourite. Not only was Walter the foreman at Harry Skirrow's workshop and the works' driver but he was also a near neighbour of George Turvey. In fact, it had been Walter who introduced George to Midget Car Racing. Without a doubt George was racing in the best Midget Car in the country. Vic made a good start in the race and in a thrilling duel beat George by about three lengths. Vic Patterson was now the 1937 Midget Car Champion of Great Britain and walked away with the top prize money and his share of the £500.

Above: Londoner George Turvey was an electrical contractor by trade who had dabbled competitively in both bikes and cars before finding his forte with Midget Cars.

Left: Vic Patterson started his Midget Car career after seeing the Midgets race at Barnet speedway in 1935. During the early phase of his career he shared a car with Spike Rhiando.

Apart from a couple of battles the racing hadn't been as close as had been hoped; nevertheless the mere fact that it was a championship carried the event. The inquest after the meeting boded well for the Manchester drivers. Charlie Pashley's performances in his revamped car had been a revelation. When Charlie obtained his new JAP engine there wasn't a great deal of spanner work to do. The engine was inserted in the same location as the old two stoke, being placed east west in a similar way as engines were fitted to three-wheeled Morgans. This logical move meant that the drive from the JAP coupled up directly with the Eltos prop shaft and although it looked rather odd and cumbersome it worked well. As with all good racers Charlie looked for ways to improve the car further. Now that he had more time he tried the engine north south, the same way as the Skirrows. This involved a lot more fabrication; the rear axle was altered and chain drive installed. The advantage of this was that sprockets could be changed to allow different gearings for different tracks. After this little bit of experimentation Charlie decided that the original idea was best; it meant far less work. The theory of playing around with sprockets wasn't as great an advantage as was first thought.

The day after Belle Vue's big event Marsh, Worswick and a delighted Pashley were at Coventry. It was a bit of an anti-climax for everyone; even the cars struggled! The meeting was blighted by motor trouble, the previous night's racing having taken its toll on the car mechanics. The week after their away day in London the bikes were back at Manchester. There was no room on the programme for the Midget Cars as Hyde Road

Amongst the many changes that Charlie Pashley tried was fitting the JAP engine in a conventional north/south manner, but this proved less successful. (Rod Pashley collection)

A great deal has been written about the charismatic Spike but his actual background was far different from the persona he portrayed.

was playing host to one of the most important speedway meetings at Hyde Road; a motorcycle speedway test match between England and Australia. Although the cars had had a two week break, Lea Bridge and Coventry still offered bookings. The triumph of the British Championship encouraged Car Speedways to follow suit. Coventry presented the Midlands Championship and Lea Bridge the Southern Speedway Car Championship. Neither of these tracks had the same financial power as Belle Vue. Nevertheless a very sizeable reward of £200 was put up for each event. Mackereth and Rhiando made up for their disappointment at Manchester; Walter became the Midland Champion and Spike the Southern Champion. This time the championships were held over the standard twenty heats. Once again Charlie Pashley's new car went well, particularly at Lea Bridge, where he finished with a very commendable eleven points to place him fourth.

When the cars returned to Manchester for their allotted Saturday night slot it was once again just one race. To keep interest buzzing Spence needed to come up with original ideas. All sorts of novelty races were invented and one of the most bizarre took place on 10 July. Eight cars were to race over ten laps. The eight drivers were the regular Manchester chaps, Worswick, Pashley, Marsh, Warburton and Cooper, plus the return of champions Vic Patterson and Walter Mackereth. The eighth driver was Charles Gaffin who was taking part in his first contest, but tragically this was to be Gaffin's only competitive race. There was a twist about the start as it was neither a clutch start nor rolling start, and the cars lined up off the track and just behind the white line. The drivers stood a few yards behind the cars. When the starter dropped the flag the drivers sprinted to their cars jumped in and were pushed away! This was a chaotic and dangerous start procedure which the spectators thoroughly enjoyed. Pashley and Worswick were first away. Pashley was able to maintain his lead and won. Worswick, though, couldn't hang on to second and was passed by Mackereth and Patterson.

The ease with which Mackereth and Patterson had passed Worswick showed that the Belle Vue drivers needed an urgent replacement for the Elto engine. If they wished to compete on a level playing field with the Skirrows then 8/80 engines JAP needed to be fitted as soon as possible to the other cars. Pashley had shown that with this engine they would be able to compete on equal terms. The faith that Spence had put in Pashley's development skills was about to pay off. There was now a scramble to acquire the 8/80s and get them fitted into the Eltos. Strictly speaking the cars that Len Hulme had built could now hardly be called Eltos. The chassis was built in Ardwick and the only true Elto part had been the engine. In future when the new re-engined cars appeared they were programmed as 'American JAPs'.

Midget Cars now followed the same path that motorcycle speedway had taken a few years previous. League racing was now up and running; not with the expected numbers, as had been first hoped, but with just four teams at two tracks. With Belle Vue declining to join in, it meant that the Hyde road based drivers could link up with any of the four teams. Accordingly they could have regular racing at least twice a

---

★ *The* ★

GREATEST CINDER SHOW IN LONDON!

Setting a new Standard in Spectacle!

MIDGET CAR RACING

Provinces :

SQUIB BURTON
STAN MILLS
SID PLEVIN
BRUCE WARBURTON
FRANK BULLOCK
JIMMY RAYNES

Lea Bridge :

SPIKE RHIANDO
ERIC WORSWICK
CHAS. PASHLEY
SID MARTIN
STAN JORGENSON
BASIL DE MATTOS

at **LEA BRIDGE SPEEDWAY**

EVERY WEDNESDAY at 8.15 p.m.

See the NEW LEAGUE CHAMPIONS NEXT WEEK:

PROVINCES v. LEA BRIDGE

in the First Round of the Midget Car National Trophy Competition

also "TRY-OUT" INTER-TEAM RACE   CAPTAIN'S MATCH RACE   SCRATCH EVENTS

Admission 1s. 3d., 1s. 6d., 2s. 6d.   Children 6d.   Car Park.   Refreshments.

Eric Worswick and Chas Pashley gain top billing for the Lea Bridge team.

week. The decision as to which drivers joined what teams is unknown; probably the decision was made by Baxter and the Car Speedways directors. The teams had been chosen in such a way that no one team would dominate; careful selection had made them as equal as possible. It also meant that the Manchester squad found themselves in different teams. Charlie Pashley and Eric Worswick became members of the Lea Bridge team. Wimslow's Frank Marsh became a Londoner. Bruce Warburton was enrolled into the Coventry team, where he joined fellow Northerners Syd Plevin and Joe Wildblood. Tommy Cooper decided not to join any team, being content to race at just Manchester.

The mini league kicked off at Coventry on 18 July, with Frank Marsh making his debut for the London team. Three days later it was the turn of Lea Bridge to race against the Provinces. This match turned out to be a remarkable meeting for Eric Worswick. Eric ended the match with a splendid eleven points. Eric's car was now fitted with a new 8/80 1000cc JAP engine and this just proved what an inspirational choice it was. If further proof were needed that all Eric needed was a decent car, then his performance in Heat 4 proved the point. In this race he knocked 0.6 seconds off Spike Rhiando's track record. This feat now elevated him to the realm of star driver, the one the competitors wanted to beat.

Even though Belle Vue hadn't joined the mini league, nor had they presented Midget Car racing after the motorcycle speedway meetings for a while, they hadn't completely abandoned Midget Car racing. The Belle Vue Aces motorcycle speedway team was packed with many international stars. If any one of them was injured or on international duty they needed to be replaced with capable riders. Because of this they had a huge squad of riders all of whom needed competitive track time. To give these lesser lights track time, and to keep them happy, they rode for Liverpool in a lower division. Unfortunately crowds at Liverpool were not good enough and the venue closed its doors. Spence wanted his reserve team to continue. To enable them to fulfil their remaining fixtures he moved the whole team back to Hyde Road where a new name and race night was needed. Spence decided that Thursday evening was the best day, wisely changing their name to 'Belle Vue Mersysiders'. To give these second division meetings a bit more interest Spence moved the Midget Cars from Saturday to Thursday. The first of these new dates was 22 July, the day after Eric Worswick had broken the Lea Bridge track record. Seven cars turned up to race over ten laps and the dangerous 'run to your cars' start was dispensed with and replaced by the normal rolling start. Regrettably Eric was unable to show off his new car. Marsh, Warburton and Cooper had not yet obtained their JAP engines and were all stuck with their Eltos. Harry Skirrow, Vic Patterson and Les White came up from London to join in. Les had replaced his Salmson Special with the very latest four-wheel drive Skirrow, a car that he had purchased on special terms, quickly paying off the balance out of his winnings. The race was won by Charlie Pashley in his American JAP. Harry Skirrow come home second with Les White who was rapidly getting the hang of four-wheel drive, third.

The following Thursday, Pashley and Worswick went head to head in a match race; and what a race this turned out to be! Both drivers were in identical cars, neither one of them having an unfair advantage. At the end of four laps Eric had lowered Rhiandos' track record to 78.2 seconds. Eric had equalled the fastest time that Eric Langton, one of the 'Aces' top riders, had put up at the previous Saturday's speedway meeting. Over the next couple of weeks both Worswick and Pashley made solo attempts at the track record, but neither of them was able to beat the record. Worswick could only manage 79 seconds and Pashley was only 0.2 of a second quicker in 78.8. Lack of track time in Manchester wasn't a problem for the local drivers, as they were continuing to race every week elsewhere. They did all come together in the last Thursday in August when Pashley had the edge over Worswick and Warburton.

The first few weeks in September were lean times for the Midgets at Hyde Road as only two four-wheel events took place. The first was the appearance of Faye Taylour who gave a four lap demonstration of her skills. Faye was a lady motor sport enthusiast from Ireland. Much has been written about her career; from her early years as the best female motorcycle speedway rider in the UK, through to her speedcar exploits in Australia during the fifties. The second September event was a match race which took place after the Belle Vue 'Merseysiders' had beaten Nottingham. Now that the Midget Car league was in full swing there were days when some drivers had some spare time; e.g. if Lea Bridge were racing Coventry or the Provences then those drivers in the London team had a day off. So when the London team weren't racing at Lea Bridge Frank Marsh had a free week. Frank made use of his time off and competed in a race against Bill Kitchen. Bill hadn't raced Midgets for a while and it showed as Frank won fairly easily.

League racing at the Car Speedway tracks was proving to be a winner. Drivers were paid per point plus start money; no points meant less prize money. As a consequence of this they were chasing every point. The incentive of earning extra money no doubt pushed some drivers beyond their natural limit resulting in spectacular crashes. More

The Irish lady racing car driver Faye Taylour managed to make a living travelling the world racing both bikes and cars.

Six-foot-two car salesman Bruce Warburton was involved with the Manchester Midgets from the very start.

often than not accidents happened when drivers became tangled up in someone else's mistake. One particularly nasty crash that happened at Coventry ended Tommy Sullman's career and photographs of the pile-up appeared in the next day's daily newspapers. Stylised images of this photo were used by the Belle Vue publicity team to illustrate an advertisement for their next Midget Car meeting. One particular Manchester driver who was having a torrid time was Provinces' team member Bruce Warburton. On consecutive weeks during August he unluckily smashed into the fence and was stretchered off both times.

By the first week in September all the league fixtures had been completed. It was Bruce Warburton's team The Provinces who were crowned league champions. Bruce ably backed up the established stars in his team; putting in some sterling performances. He saved his best feat for the very last league match. Provinces needed to defeat Coventry to clinch the title; Bruce rose to the occasion with a resounding 10 points Wishing to continue with team racing, Car Speedways came up with the idea of a knock-out competition. Instead of just one meeting the first round was on a home and away basis; the team with the highest aggregate score being the winner. The first rounds of the competition began at Coventry on 15 September followed by Lea Bridge four days later; other rounds were to take place on 22 and 26 September. In between these dates Belle Vue were preparing for another of their stupendous nights.

Crowd safety was not a priority and it was up to the spectators to get out of the way of runaway cars. Here they dash in all directions when they see Bruce Warburton's car heading towards them.

The winning Provinces team pose for their victory photograph. From left to right they Are, Jimmy Raynes, Frank Bullock, Bruce Warburton, Squib Burton, Stan Mills, Syd Plevin and Joe Wildblood. (Courtesy of Doug Wildblood)

Extra entertainment was added to the programme in the hope that it would entice more spectators to come along.

On the last Saturday in September the Belle Vue 'Aces' were once again racing away at Harringay. This free date allowed the Midgets to return for another prestigious individual meeting. There had been a Midland Championship, a Southern Drivers Championship and the British Championship. With Manchester being in the North of England then the obvious name for the competition was 'The Speedway Car Championship of the North'. To make the meeting even more memorable Belle Vue's superb publicity department swung into action. The company that ran the Pleasure Gardens had several skilled sign writers who kept the art work on the rides and side shows in tip top condition. These people were responsible for the lurid drawings on the Ghost Train, Bumper Cars etc, and their idea of advertising the next meeting was to show stylised Midget Cars upside down and piling into the fence! Not all the publicity was that dramatic; on the night of the meeting Manchester's *Evening Chronicle* was giving away well produced prints of new local hero Eric Worswick.

Once again sixteen of the best drivers were invited along. Five of the Belle Vue drivers, Cooper, Marsh, Pashley, Warburton and Worswick were all driving the Len Hulme American JAPs. By now every one of them had dumped the Evinrude two-stroke engine and converted their cars to take the JAP 8/80 V-twin. Once Charlie Pashley was satisfied with the best set up; he helped convert all the other American JAPs to the east west configuration. One other conversion that was carried out was to fit the cars with dog clutches. Also on the race card were a couple of standard Eltos. These two

A SPLENDID

SOUVENIR ART PHOTOGRAPH of

Eric Worswick

is presented Free with the **Evening Chronicle**
on Sale in the Speedway to-night

• •

Handsome Glossed Portraits of your favourite
riders will be presented at the Speedway,
every Saturday with the

Evening Chronicle

during the Racing Season.

Seizing an opportunity to increase sales the *Evening Chronicle* joined forces with Belle Vue to promote both the newspaper and the speedway.

cars were to be driven by 'Acorn' Dobson and Fred Alexander, who was making a rare return to Belle Vue. Neither of them featured in the main event as both of them were listed as reserves. When the programme went to press Les White was down to drive his Salmsom Special, except by now he was getting to grips with his new Skirrow. All the other cars, excluding Jimmy Raynes' Sullman Anzani, were also the four-wheel drive Skirrows. These were driven by Midland Champion Walter Mackereth, British Champion Vic Patterson and Southern Champion Spike Rhiando. Making up the rest of the field were Southern domiciled drivers Syd Emery, Ron Wills, George Turvey and Val Atkinson. Val was originally from Westmoreland. When Harry Skirrow relocated his Midget Car building project Val, together with Walter Mackereth and Johnny Young, also moved South. All three of them had been employees at Skirrow's Ambleside garage. The final driver in the line-up was Squib Burton who was making a return to Hyde Road. Squib needed no introduction to the Belle Vue regulars. Before injury had forced him into retirement he had been one of the country's top motorcycle speedway riders.

The meeting was over sixteen heats meaning that each driver had only four races. Traditionally these individual meetings were usually held over twenty heats. Knocking four heats off the championship allowed the meeting to finish earlier than normal.

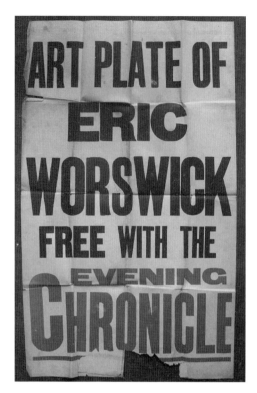

Posters were on display in the newspapers' billboards at every meeting. (Courtesy of Clive Worswick)

This allowed the management put on extra entertainment in the form of the Army's Royal Signals Motorcycle Display Team. The opening heat of the championship set the standard for the rest on the night. Walter Mackereth lowered the track record to 78.6 seconds. In this opening heat he was pushed all the way by Eric Worswick who sat on his tail waiting in vain for an opening or for Walter to make a mistake. British Champion Vic Patterson's chances of repeating his earlier success took a severe dent as he could only manage third. Heat six highlighted just how hard everyone was trying when Eric Worswick equalled Mackereth's new track record. No matter how much the other drivers tried no one was able to get near to Walter, who walked away with the championship, scoring a faultless twelve points. The Skirrow cars didn't have things all their own way. Eric Worswick's Manchester built American JAP was a match for everyone except Walter; he finished second with eleven points. Third place went to veteran Ron Wills; Ron had been one of the pioneers of Midget Car racing. He had been competing since 1934; although Ron had won races before this was the best result that he had ever achieved. Charlie Pashley could well have finished in the medals but heats ten and fifteen spoiled his chances. Third place in the championship was perhaps decided in heat ten, when Ron Wills finished ahead of Charlie. A third place in heat fifteen, behind the unstoppable Mackereth and playboy Londoner Syd Emery ended his chances. Frank Marsh and Tommy Cooper performed reasonably well in their new cars. Bruce Warburton was very disappointed with just one point; the only person he managed to beat was Stan Mills in heat eight.

There were only three more weeks before the stadium brought down the shutters on the 1937 season. Midget Cars didn't feature in any of these meetings, the Northern Car Championship being the zenith of their season. During those last three weeks Lea Bridge and Coventry likewise brought their season to an end with individual events and the conclusion of the knock-out competition. The very last meeting of the season was at Coventry on 18 October and all the Manchester men featured. The main event was the second leg of the KO cup final. This was between the league champions, The Provences, and the less popular London team. After the aggregate scores were added up it was The Provences who once again came out on top, the three Northern team members all contributing well towards the Provence's victory.

The curtain now came down on the 1937 season and it was time to reflect on how the events of the past year had gone. Midget Car racing had expanded and was now quite capable of standing on its own feet. This was particularly so now that Car Speedways had been able to stage weekly meetings at Coventry and Lea Bridge. Belle Vue had also shown that the Manchester public were quite prepared to turn up and support meetings purely for Midget Cars. Perhaps the only black spot was Glasgow which closed its doors to the Midgets after about ten meetings. The cars too had improved beyond all recognition. There had been no doubting the competitiveness of the Elto cars, especially in the USA. Here in the UK things were a little different with the track

Twin rear wheels were tried in the hope of gaining an extra advantage over the more conventional set up.

surfaces being the problem. The hard sun-baked tracks of California and the oiled dirt tracks of the other parts of the United States were ideal surfaces for the screaming two-stroke engine. In the UK the tracks were covered with black ash, essentially cinders derived from industrial waste. It was this loose surface that held back the Eltos especially after other cars started to employ four-wheel drive. To gain a little extra grip some of the Manchester drivers fitted twin wheels to the rear axles. This wasn't as effective as hoped as the extra width and weight of the rear tyres impeded broadsiding around the turns. The greatest improvement to the Northern cars came about when they fitted the JAP engines. On their day the top north west drivers were a match for anyone. Regular racing had defiantly put an edge on their performances, as witnessed by Eric Worswicks' track records. To bring on and encourage new talent, Belle Vue held regular practice sessions. Not many of those taking part in the trials actually made it onto the Saturday or Thursday's race card. One who had managed it was John Gaffin but unfortunately his promising career ended tragically when he was involved in a fatal road accident the week after he had made his debut. New faces appeared, and just as quickly vanished, especially when the newcomers recognised the commitment that was necessary to be a proficient driver. One driver, Fred Alexander, had shown great potential. So keen had Fred been to take up the sport that he had even gone ahead and purchased a Len Hulme Elto. After some good results he drifted from the Belle Vue scene. He and his car returned to his home track at Norwich, where after doing a few demonstrations, he promptly put it up for sale. His asking price was £225, how much he paid for the car is not known, but the previous year Hulme was selling his brand new Eltos for £195. In other parts of the country a promising sign had been the number of competitive drivers that were emerging; which boded well for the future.

There was however one big blot on the landscape and that was the motorcycle faction. The Speedway Control Board was not at all happy with Speedway riders taking part in Midget Car Racing. During the previous year the board had banned riders who were under contract to the various Speedway Teams from taking part in Midget Car Racing. After a little pressure the Board did relent and allowed riders to race but only on the tracks that held their contracts. This rule meant that Bill Kitchen and 'Acorn' Dobson could only race at Belle Vue. Further subtle pressure was being put on the Midget Car scene by the Speedway press. Towards the end of 1937 the magazine *Speedway News* carried a feature outlining their policy towards Midget Car Racing. 'We have no prejudices against this type of racing. On the contrary it is undeniably interesting and even thrilling to watch, and we wish it to progress. But it is, at the moment, more or less an "unrecognised" sport. It appears to lack an unbiased governing body, such as speedway racing has in the ACU and the whole of the meetings, arrangements, appointment of stewards, judges, time-keepers and other officials seem to lie in the hands of those commercially interested.' They went on to suggest that the control of the sport should pass into the hands of the RAC and out of the influence of those who held the commercial rights. They probably feared that business-related interests would over-rule fair play. 'So recently as last week all speedway promoters were advised by the ACU that they must not allow miniature car racing either before or during a motorcycle meeting. We understand that this action is directly due to protests from riders, who consider that the use of small cars makes surfaces dangerous for the purpose originally intended.' This form of blackmail by the two-wheeled whingers was not going to have too much effect on those behind Midget Car Racing. They were after all hard-nosed business men who were not going to be pushed around by a group of unpaid amateurs from the ACU establishment.

Chapter 6

Indian Summer

1938 was to be the year when Midget Car racing became a regular and established form of motor racing in the UK. Optimism was high; especially as at the end of the previous year when a leading motor racing journal published a glowing endorsement of the sport by none other than Cecil Kimber, the managing director of the MG Car Co. Ltd. The piece said that Kimber, '...has announced his opinion that in a few years' time he expects "Doodle Bug" racing to concentrate all public interest and that it will be far more thrilling to watch than Grand Prix racing'.

During the winter of 1937/38 all the plans and ideas came to fruition. Throughout the winter meetings and discussions had taken place between several interested parties. The most significant result of these talks was that a National League was to be formed to promote Midget Car Racing; and one of the teams who were to join the league was Belle Vue. One of the first things that the interested parties did was to set up a board of control that would coordinate and organise Midget Car racing. The board consisted of Jimmy Baxter, Harry Skirrow, Tom Bradbury-Pratt, Charles Knott, Alex Jackson, Ron Hewitt, Victor Martin and Belle Vue supremo E. O. Spence. All of these members had business-related interests in Midget Cars and motorcycle Speedway. Baxter and Skirrow controlled Coventry and Lea Bridge, Bradbury-Pratt and Knott were the partners who ran Southampton Speedway. Alex Jackson was the manager of the Wembley Lions speedway team. Ron Hewitt was in advanced negotiations with a track in the Midlands. Victor Martin had connections with the engine manufacturers, JAP, as well as owning the workshops where Harry Skirrow manufactured his Midget Cars. Spence's seat on the Board of Control confirmed that Belle Vue were totally committed in their desire to see Midget Car Racing recognised as a national motor sport. The above members now set about overhauling the whole system of promoting Midget Cars.

The first thing these members did was to name their organization the National Association of Speedway Car Racing Circuits Ltd. (NASCRC). They appointed several competent and experienced Race Stewards to adjudicate and control race meetings. These stewards saw to it that meetings were run in accordance with the new rules that the Board had laid down. The rules were written down and published in a small booklet that could be purchased for 6d (2 1/2p). These rules consisted of everything from the duties of the stewards, team size, car dimensions, racing conduct and many

THE ASSOCIATION OF SPEEDWAY CAR RACING CIRCUITS
LIMITED.

With the Secretary's Compliments

BUCHANAN BUILDINGS,

24, HOLBORN, E.C.1.

TELEPHONE:

HOLBORN 7391

In their affairs the governing body always presented a professional outlook.

other details relating to the smooth running of Midget Car Racing. One fact relating to the appearance of those taking part was that drivers '…shall at all times provide themselves with clean white overalls'. The control board intended to show the rest of the motor racing world that they were a smart professionally run organisation who would not tolerate shoddy presentation.

A universal pay structure was also implemented. To help drivers with their expenses they were guaranteed at least £3 per meeting, no matter how poorly they had performed. For league matches team members earned 15s (75p) a point. For second-half events, where it was an individual's performance that counted, a driver was paid 10/- (50p) appearance money. As an incentive a bonus of £1 was paid to the winner of every heat. For those that managed to win through to a final the prize money was £4 for first place £3 for second and so on down to last.

The whole administration of the NASCRC was conducted from offices situated in the Holborn district of London. The entire set up was to be administered by Guy Hopkins. Guy was employed as a permanent secretary; his duties included overseeing every aspect of the organization. He was also responsible for processing driver's applications and issuing them with the appropriate competition licences. Upon registration of their licences the drivers were given a racing number which they had to display on their cars for the whole season. At the start of the season six tracks came forward to form a National Midget Car League. Six teams was a very healthy number, considering that

THE NATIONAL ASSOCIATION OF SPEEDWAY CAR RACING CIRCUITS, LTD.

BUCHANAN BUILDINGS,
24, HOLBORN, LONDON, E.C.1.

No. 38/ **16**

Fee Paid £— :/0 : 0

LICENCE TO DRIVE

UNDER THE RULES OF THE N.A.S.C.R.C.

(Valid to the 31st December, 1938)

Issued to Mr *Frank Marsh*

Under the approved assumed name of ....

Permanent Address *Knutsford Road Garage,*
Wilmslow, Cheshire

Car No. *68*

Given at *London* the *22nd* day of *April* 1938.

Geo Hopkins

Holder's Signature *Frank Marsh*   Secretary

All drivers had to hold a valid licence to compete on the dirt tracks.

the Motorcycle Speedway National League was made up of only seven teams. Midget Car teams were to consist of six drivers with team matches being over twelve heats. The well-established motorcycle speedway format of four drivers per heat, two from each team, was implemented. All team races were over four laps, the winner gaining three points, the second two points and third just one. The points from each heat were carried forward to the next, and obviously at the end of the twelve heats the team with the highest running total was declared the winner and gained two league points. A draw would mean one point each. It was planned that each team would race ten home and ten away league matches i.e. they would race each team twice, both at home and away. The six tracks who set out to show the doubters that Midget Car Racing was here to stay were Southampton, Wembley, Lea Bridge, Coventry, Leicester and Belle Vue. Southampton, Wembley and Belle Vue were established motorcycle speedway tracks and as such had to share their track with the bikes. It was up to the promoters of these tracks to arrange their Midget Car commitments around the bike schedules. The other three tracks could run Midget Car meetings every week without having to fit in and work around other fixtures. Six teams with six drivers per team meant that at least thirty-six drivers were needed. After taking away the six Belle Vue personnel it meant that thirty drivers had to be conjured up. It was doubtful if that number of capable drivers were around in early 1938. To overcome this problem a certain amount of lateral thinking was needed. The promoters sat down and decided to implement a driver equalisation scheme. Star drivers were shared out amongst the other five clubs and to overcome the lack of cars promoters encouraged car sharing. It was hoped that once the season was under way new drivers would come forward to fill the ranks. Belle Vue were in the lucky position of having a core of experienced drivers; as yet there was no need for them to take drivers from other tracks. Furthermore they had the luxury of having enough cars to field a team. Although there were no strict contractual agreements between drivers and teams, as there was in motorcycle speedway, it was expected that drivers assigned to the various teams would remain there throughout the season. What was supposed to happen and what actually happened were two different things. The paying public seemed happy to go along with the explanations and excuses that the promoters gave when drivers were switched from one track to another.

Wisely the league was not due to begin until well into the new season. This allowed tracks to train up new talent and assess who was available. Belle Vue had no plans to run Midget Car meetings until later in the season, nor any plans to stage the occasional race after the motorcycle speedway meetings. The lack of racing on their home track didn't mean that the Manchester drivers had to hang around and wait for their season to start, as drivers were in demand and there was plenty of racing to be had on the other tracks. This lack of track action didn't mean there was no Midget Car activity at Hyde Road; on the contrary trials and practice sessions continued apace. These trials were put on during the early part of the season. The day chosen for the practice sessions was Wednesday afternoon which incidentally was early closing day for Manchester's stores. The public were invited to come along and watch; no doubt they would have been urged to visit the Pleasure Gardens after the trials where they would be encouraged to spend their cash on the numerous attractions.

The season opened on Good Friday at Southampton's Banister Court Stadium. This was Southampton's very first all Midget Car meeting, after having previously put on the occasional race after the motorcycle speedway meetings. The meeting was a Best Pairs competition with every track being represented. Wembley sent along Ron Wills and Syd Plevin; Lea Bridge, Spike Rhiando and Syd Emery. Leicester's pair was Squib Burton and Gene Crowley, Walter Mackereth and George Turvey represented Coventry. The home pair was Les White and Jimmy Raynes. Manchester's top two drivers, Eric Worswick and Charlie Pashley, made the long trip to the South coast to be the Belle Vue representatives. Just in case any driver had a problem then Basil deMattos and 'Skid' Martin were on hand to fill in as reserves. The meeting was well supported with the local press claiming that 11,000 spectators watched this, '...first Speedway motor-car racing meeting'. They saw Coventry's Walter Mackereth and George Turvey carry off the trophy. The Belle Vue duo struggled among the top talent of the Midget Car world; they finished last with a collective three points. The only opposing drivers that they managed to beat were Jimmy Raynes and Gene Crowley. It was not that the Belle Vue boys had suddenly become poor drivers; the year before their JAP-engined cars had broken track records at Belle Vue and Lea Bridge. It was the fact that during the winter the Skirrow specials had been upgraded. A slight relocation of the engine, the fitting of tie rods and a new body shape had made the Skirrow a much better car. The opening meeting had gone well with plenty of thrills and spills. The only unfortunate incident had been a mishap that involved Wembley's veteran driver Ron Wills. Ron broke a collar bone when he crashed through the safety fence and ended up on Banister Court's greyhound track. The crash caused quite a bit of damage to the dog track. The stadium owners were furious and immediately forced promoters Bradbury-Pratt and Knott to rethink their obligations to Midget Car racing. The following week's Southampton Car Championship was called off. Rather than jeopardise their motorcycle speedway interests they felt that they had no option but to withdraw Southampton from the Midget Car league. This early blow could well have derailed the league's plans. The Midget Car Association took this disappointment it in its stride as they still had five tracks committed to the league. The withdrawal of Southampton did have one positive effect as it meant that drivers that had been assigned to them were now available to drive for other teams. This eased the pressure on fellow promoters in their search to find the extra drivers that were needed.

Both Coventry and Lea Bridge began their racing season over the Easter weekend. Coventry ran every Sunday and Lea Bridge every Monday. Amongst the usual drivers who regularly took part were the Manchester based drivers. Two of them, Pashley and Worswick, had a particularly hectic weekend in May. Having vowed never to return to Scotland, on Saturday 16 May they accepted a booking to give a demonstration. This time it was to race at Edinburgh's Marine Gardens and not Glasgow's White City. After the Saturday night demonstration it was down to Coventry for Sunday's afternoon meeting followed by London's Lea Bridge on Monday evening. Considering the pre-war roads and the vehicles of the time Manchester to Edinburgh, back to Manchester then on to Coventry and on down to London before returning back to Manchester late on Monday night, was quite a feat!

The demonstration at Edinburgh must have gone down well as both Eric and Charlie were invited back in June for more duels. It could just be possible that those involved with the demonstrations were hoping to persuade Edinburgh to put together a team to compete in the league; which was being hinted at in the *News Chronicle*. With a little help it would not have been too difficult for Edinburgh to raise a team; there were after all several drivers who had raced the year before at Glasgow. Nothing was to come of these overtures and Edinburgh never joined the league.

Having lost Southampton, the aspirations of the National Midget Car league was to take a further setback. Negotiations between Ron Hewitt and the owners of the Leicester Super stadium broke down as the owners decided that they didn't want Midget Car Speedway there. A disappointed Hewitt looked around for another venue. His search took him to Stoke-on-Trent; here he was able to come to an agreement with the owners of Hanley's Sun Street stadium. Commencing in July Hewitt was able to put on regular Midget Car meetings every Thursday night. Drivers that had been allocated to Leicester were now transferred to Stoke.

The Car Speedways' tracks of Coventry and Lea Bridge had been giving licenced drivers plenty of competition. With so much racing taking place it was inevitable that there would be lots of crashes. The Manchester drivers were no exception and suffered their fair share of mishaps. One of the most spectacular accidents that could well have ended in tragedy befell Eric Worswick. Eric was competing in the Tommy Sullman

Track staff helps to manoeuvre Eric Worswick's car back onto the track, while Eric calms his nerves by taking a few puffs on his pipe. (Courtesy of Clive Worswick)

Trophy at Coventry. In heat fifteen Tony Hulme over-slid on one of the bends and right behind him was Eric Worswick. Eric's car collided with Hulme's car and was catapulted into the air. The *Midland Daily Telegraph* claimed that, '…The car had travelled nearly 20 yards in the air and must have passed over the heads of several spectators before striking the ground again. The car landed on its wheels ran on a couple of yards and skidded round to a standstill on a spot where a few seconds before there had been a crowd'. Eric was unscathed, but several spectators had to be attended to by members of the St John's Ambulance Brigade. There was however one very serious injury to a sixteen-year-old lad who suffered a broken thigh and was rushed to Coventry hospital. In those far off days when Health and Safety was not such an issue spectators attended race meetings *at their own risk*. Before the war *at their own risk* meant precisely that, hence no litigation or inquiry followed this incident.

The Belle Vue based drivers had been involved with team racing for a while. One thing that they had never experienced was representing their city in a team event at Hyde Road. This was to change on Saturday 10 June. With the Belle Aces racing away at Harringay it was decided to stage a Midget Car team match. Rather than take on one of the new league teams, Belle Vue opted to race against a team selected from the top drivers in the country. This opening team event, Belle Vue verses The Rest, was a canny move on Spence's behalf. The team that was to represent 'The Rest' was made up

Tension is high before the start of the meeting as drivers and mechanics mill around their cars. (Rod Pashley collection)

of some the finest drivers in the country. If Belle Vue were to lose heavily against such a powerful team then they would have the knowledge that they would never meet such a strong opposition again. The trials and the practice sessions that had taken place had, as yet, not found drivers who could compete effectively against the more established drivers. In choosing six drivers for their opening team event Belle Vue applied a certain amount of latitude. The four stalwarts who had been representing Manchester were obvious choices and Pashley, Worswick, Warburton and Marsh formed the backbone of the team. With no other local drivers available they seconded the ebullient Syd Emery and elder statesman Ron Wills. The new rules of Midget Car team racing allowed the teams to nominate a seventh reserve driver. In a team match the reserve driver didn't have a programmed drive; instead he could take the place of one of his team mates at any time. The man chosen to fill this berth was Billy Murden. Although never a star driver; Billy was one of those keen competitors who would take his car anywhere for a drive. In 1936, together with Ian St'Nairn, he even went over to Sweden to give a demonstration at Stockholm's Solvana Trotting track. The other team was packed with the very best drivers in the country. Coventry's captain, Walter Mackereth was paired with Wembley captain, Les White. Stoke's top driver, Squib Burton, lined up with teenage sensation, Johnny Young. The final pair were the unforgettable Spike Rhiando and Stan Mills. At reserve was the 1937 British Champion Vic Patterson. This was a formidable team and it is doubtful if Belle Vue would ever come up against such

In 1935 at the Solvana trotting track nr Stockholm Billy Murden averaged nearly 56 mph here he leads Ian StNairn who is driving his rear engine Midget.

strong opposition again. On the night of the meeting an earlier injury to Syd Emery prevented him from fulfilling this engagement; in his place came Val Atkinson. Val was relatively new to racing but not to Midget Cars. Ever since Harry Skirrow started to manufacture his Midget Cars, Val had been part of the team that assembled them. Ron Wills too was unable to make the trip and his place was taken by Skid Martin. Skid Martin's background was unique; he was a professional stunt driver who decided that the challenge of Midget Car Racing was too great a challenge to ignore.

In an action packed meeting 'The Rest' won by 37 points to 34; a very good result for Belle Vue considering the class of their rivals. The opening race was sensational and the track was in perfect condition. Previously the Midget car races had taken place at the end of motorcycle speedway meetings when the track had been badly cut up but this time the track had a perfect racing surface. Walter Mackereth's winning time in the first heat smashed Eric Worswick's track record. He knocked an astonishing 1.6 seconds off Worswick's best time leaving it at 76.6 seconds. Walters' winning time was now comparable to that of the bikes. During the previous week's motorcycle speedway meeting the fastest time of the night had been 78.0 seconds. Even allowing for the rolling start, the cars were now just as rapid around the Belle Vue track as the bikes. This was something that Spence had hoped would happen when he first started staging Midget Car racing four years before. Midget Car Racing had now come of age and could stand on its own feet; no longer could the distractors claim that the cars were not as quick. The drivers had now mastered the art of backing their cars into the turns; flying into the bends sideways was the norm. As soon as the flag dropped they really

Louis Klemantansky was in the right place to capture this dramatic shot after Les White had clipped the wheel of Eric Worswick.

went for it. No quarter was asked nor given; if a gap appeared they dived in, and with such competitive racing accidents were bound to occur. The inevitable happened in heat four. On the first bend of the first lap Les White's car touched the near front wheel of Eric Worswick's car, causing White's car to roll over. Standing on the inside of the track was a budding photographer who captured the moment. The photographer was Louis Klemantansky who went on to become a legend in the world of motor racing photography, and the image he captured became one of the iconic pictures of Midget Car Racing in the UK. The photo was used to plug the thrills and spills of the sport and appeared in advertisements to promote other tracks. Later in the meeting a further incident took place which showed how much more dangerous Midget Car Racing was compared to the bikes. Having realised this, the maintenance staff at Belle Vue had constructed an extra safety barrier behind the normal speedway fence. When the cars took to the track spectators were told to stand behind this extra protective barrier. Unless this area was continually patrolled, spectators (especially small boys) would sneak in to take a closer look at the action. In heat nine the inevitable happened when an eleven-year-old boy crept into this no go area. When Skid Martin was trying to avoid an over sliding Eric Worswick he smacked into the safety fence. The wooden fence snapped in a couple of places scattering debris, unhappily one of these pieces struck the unfortunate boy who was injured.

The performance of the four regulars was heartening and boded well for the future; Eric Worswick and an inspired Frank Marsh were the top scorers. Eric's eight points would certainly have been higher but the steward of the meeting disqualified him for

'Ten Ton' Syd Emery, as he was affectionately known by the Manchester   Supporters, tries out an Elto at Lea Bridge.

causing the race to be stopped. Frank also had a good night with a win, two seconds and a third. Three weeks later, on 7 July, Frank was to write his name in the annals of British Midget Car history. On that day a story was created that was to become a legend. Meanwhile, before this date there was the important task of the British Midget Car League, which was to begin at Coventry on Sunday 11 June.

Coventry's first league match saw them defeat Lea Bridge; the following week it was Belle Vue's turn to take on the mighty Coventry 'Bees'. For their first league match Belle Vue were still trying to sort out who their six team members would be. The four regulars were always guaranteed a place in team; it was the other two slots that were causing the problem. Trials had been going on a pace and as yet no one was quite up to the high standard required. For the Coventry match Londoner's Syd Emery and Billy Murden were available. Syd was now fully fit and having recovered from his injury and was raring to go. Syd was very popular in Manchester and the controlling body had decided to assign both him and Billy to Belle Vue. On the day of the match Billy was again left out of the side. His replacement was the enigmatic Jock Furgusson more of whom later. Jock was a great friend of Syd and the pair of them were often seen together in all the best nightspots of London. The promise shown in Belle Vue's first team match was shattered in this first league match. Coventry walked away with the league points thrashing Belle Vue by 52 points to 20! The team performed so badly

Lea Bridge didn't have a team of creative artists to help with their advertisements. Instead of graphics they used photographs of the drivers.

that a Belle Vue driver never won a single race; it was the Coventry drivers who took the chequered flag every time. The only visiting driver to show any consistency was Charlie Pashley who managed to finish second three times. Charlie was Belle Vue's top scorer with eight points from five starts. A driver who did show a lot of promise was Jock Furgusson. He was well up with the more experienced drivers and was no way out-classed by them. Considering this was his first competitive meeting his two third places augured well for the future.

A week later Belle Vue raced their second league match; again this was an away fixture when it was down to London to take on Lea Bridge. This time they faired marginally better, gaining three more points but still losing heavily by 48 points to 23. On paper this looked to be another humiliating defeat. Their performance was not as bad as it appeared. Belle Vue started off well with Charlie Pashley winning the first race and Eric Worswick coming in third. After that respectable start it was a continual procession of the Blue and White of Lea Bridge. That was until heat eleven when Pashley and Worswick pulled back a few points when they came home first and second. Belle Vue's problem lay not with the drivers but with their cars. *Speedway World*, reported, 'The Eltos proved slow at the start and this factor may have accounted to a large extent for the poor show the visitors put up'. The Belle Vue drivers were not able to accelerate away from the start as quickly as the four-wheel drive Skirrows. This greatly hampered their performance; once they were up to speed it was very hard to fight their way through in the short four lap dashes that made up the league programme.

By early July the NASCRC announced that two new tracks, one at Stoke and the other at Wembley, were to open for league racing. Stoke, who had taken the place of Leicester, were scheduled to open on Thursday 21 July. Wembley's car season had started a week earlier with a showcase individual event dubbed the Gold Trophy Track Championship. At the start of the 1938 season Wembley were one of the tracks that had joined the National Car League. The reason for Wembley's late start was down to the timetabling of other events. It was not until the various Football Association cup competitions and the Rugby League challenge trophy had been competed for that the stadium was available for other events. As soon as the soccer and rugby seasons were over parts of the pitch were taken up and a speedway track was laid. Even then Midget Car Racing couldn't begin as the famous Wembley Lions motorcycle speedway team took preference over everything else. Furthermore in July, the organizers of Edinburgh's Marine Gardens speedway track decided to give the cars a chance. A full car meeting was booked for 2 July. Instead of an individual event a team match was arranged. At Glasgow the previous year there had been a problem with the partisan Ibrox crowd who had taken an instant dislike to the Manchester team. Rather than risk any crowd trouble the two sides were designated the Northern team and the Southern team. Five of the Northern team were Manchester based but somehow or another Belle Vue's Bruce Warburton found himself driving for the Southern team! If Bruce had been racing for the North then the whole Belle Vue team would have been on show. The Northern team was made up of Coventry-based drivers Frank Bullock and Johnny Young, plus Belle Vue's Frank Marsh, Charlie Pashley and Eric Worswick. Backing them up, and making their racing debuts were two new Manchester drivers,

The *Evening Chronicle*'s presentation souvenir postcard of Jack McCarthy. These rare collectables have since been catalogued by the Cartophilic Society of Great Britain.

George Goodley and Jack McCarthy, both of whom had come out of the practice sessions that had been held regularly at Hyde Road. Of the two Jack McCarthy was the most interesting. Jack was the brother of Red McCarthy, a Canadian ice skating legend who had been entertaining large audiences with his spectacular ice shows over at the Pleasure Gardens ice rink. It was claimed that Jack had raced Midget Cars in Canada and the USA but whether this was true or not it didn't really matter because he had been able to demonstrate the basic skills needed to handle a Midget Car. With Belle Vue's opening home league match only a few days away it was felt prudent to send both George and Jack up to Edinburgh. Here they would compete against the professional drivers that they would come up against when the serious business of league racing began.

The match was a great advert for Midget Car Racing with many a memorable performance. At the end of the twelve heats the Northern team won by 36 points to 35. The performance of the Northern team was remarkable in so much as that by heat five they were thirteen points behind the Southerners, with just 8 points to their 21. At the end of heat five things were looking even worse for the Northerners when they were down to five drivers. In this heat Jack McCarthy, who had been well up with the other drivers, attempted to overtake the opposition around the outside. Being more used to the wide-open spaces of Hyde Road the inevitable happened and he hit the safety fence. His car turned completely over rendering Jack unconscious. He sustained several superficial injuries and concussion but it was hoped that Jack's injuries wouldn't prove to be too debilitating and that he would be fit enough to take his place in Belle Vue's opening league match the following Wednesday. During the latter part of the contest the Manchester based drivers rallied to the cause and won five of the last seven heats; proving that their poor showing at Coventry and Lea Bridge wasn't as irredeemable as it had appeared a week or two before. The most remarkable race was heat nine. It was in this race that Frank Marsh's name became etched into British Midget Car history. Frank won the race in 83.8 seconds, a full two seconds faster than anyone had gone that evening. After the race Frank claimed that his throttle had stuck open! Somehow or other he had managed to wrestled his car to the finishing line; posting the fastest time of the night. Whether this was true or not will never be known, however a regular joke amongst the speedway fraternity is that if anyone records a time that was well above their norm then his fellow competitors would jokingly claim that his throttle must have stuck open! Frank's fast time still did not come up to the record time of 82.0 set by Walter Mackereth the week before but it should be noted that Walter's time was equal to that set by the motorcycle speedway riders earlier in the Scottish Open Championship in which some of world's finest riders had been taking part.

The much-awaited National Midget Car League was about to begin in Manchester. All the years of development and preparation were about to come to fruition on Wednesday 13 July when they were to open their league campaign against Coventry. The Hyde Road track was now about to present Speedway racing twice a week; Saturday night for the bikes and Wednesday night for the cars. After a long and tortuous start the Midget Car League was now looking rosy. Lea Bridge and Coventry were up and running, Wembley were to start their season in a couple of days' time,

As it was a mid-week meeting the start time was put back one hour to 8pm, allowing the public plenty of time to get there after work.

and Stoke were scheduled to open the following Thursday. Although not in the league Edinburgh had run a successful meeting; and Leeds too were about to stage an all car meeting. A week before the Belle Vue opener all this optimism took a bit of a knock when *Speedway World* declared, 'Lea Bridge Closes'. The withdrawal of Lea Bridge could have seriously damaged the viability of the league; four teams instead of five looked distinctly shaky. All was not lost because Roy Clive, a Midget Car fan, came to the rescue. Clive decided that the now vacant Crystal Palace track was just the place to re-introduce Midget Car Racing, especially now that regular league racing could be hosted there. An agreement was reached with Baxter and Skirrow which allowed all of the Lea Bridge assets to be transferred south of the river to the Sydenham track.

For Belle Vue's opening league match the team more or less picked itself. The squad printed in the programme was the regular four plus new trainees Goodly and McCarthy. Unfortunately McCarthy was still suffering from the injuries he had sustained at Edinburgh as his injuries were far worse than had been initially reported. It was unlikely that he would be racing for quite a while, as apart from the cuts, bruises and concussion he had also sustained a broken collar bone. In the slot vacated by McCarthy came Bill Reynolds. Unbeknown at the time Bill was to become one of the most successful Midget Car drivers that Britain had ever produced. Former dispatch rider Bill was fairly new to Midget Car Racing and first saw Midget Car Racing quite by chance when he dropped in on a practice session at Lea Bridge. With Lea Bridge now closed down he jumped at the chance to race at Belle Vue and was keen to establish himself as a leading driver.

Coventry were unbeaten in all their league matches and with all their drivers being capable of winning races, a tough challenge faced the home side. The Coventry team was led by Walter Mackereth who was ably backed by Buster Bladon, George Turvey, teenage wonder Johnny Young, ex Preston motorcycle Speedway ace Frank Chiswell

Bill found fame and fortune in Australia. So respected was his knowledge of Midget Car Racing
that after his retirement from racing that he became the resident announcer at the famous Sydney
Royal Stadium. (Terry Wright collection)

and Val Atkinson. As expected Coventry stormed into the lead and by heat six were in
the lead by 19 points to 14. The reported 8,000 spectators were to witness the finest car
meeting Manchester had seen so far. In the latter phase of the meeting Belle Vue staged
an amazing comeback; they pulled back the five point deficit, crept ahead, and won by
36 points to 33! Charlie Pashley played a captain's role, winning three of his five races
and Frank Marsh featured well as he too won three races. Again there were spectacular
prangs, all of them looking much worse than they actually were. Johnny Young hit
the fence in heat two and was thrown out of his car. In heat ten, when dicing with
two other drivers, Bill Reynolds was forced onto the grass. The *Manchester Guardian*
reported that Reynold's car, '…turned four complete somersaults'. He was thrown out
of his car and knocked unconscious but fortunately came away with nothing more
than a few broken fingers. Bill had enjoyed his experience of racing in Manchester, so
much so that after the meeting he mingled with the fans in the supporters' club before
going to hospital to have his fingers professionally attended to.

All in all it had been a good start and boded well for future Wednesday nights. The
next league match was again a home fixture this time it was to be against Wembley.
Wembley were old foes at Manchester, their motorcycle speedway team having visited
Hyde Road for many a battle. It was hoped that this great rivalry with the London
team could be transferred to the Midget Car team. Three days after the opening
league contest and just before the home match with Wembley, Charlie Pashley and
Eric Worswick made their way to the Empire Stadium for Wembley's prestigious Gold

The Gold Trophy that was won by Spike Rhiando at Wembley's one and only Midget Car meeting.

Trophy meeting. Bill Reynolds was also entered for this meeting but as he was not yet fully recovered from Wednesday's injuries he wisely decided not to race. This individual meeting was over twenty heats with each driver meeting every other driver once.

The magnificent Wembley stadium saw the mesmeric Spike Rhiando win the *Daily Sketch* sponsored Gold Trophy. The trophy was presented to him by the famous Brooklands female racing car driver Kay Petre. Spike won four of his five races; his only defeat came in heat two when he finished second behind Belle Vue's Eric Woswick. This was Eric's only heat win, in his other four races he only managed three more points, ending up with a meagre six points. Belle Vue's other representative, Charlie Pashley, went one better than Eric, scoring seven points; which included a win in heat 16 when he beat Les White, Eric Worswick and Basil deMattos.

Contemporary reports of Midget Car Racing are very sketchy and usually only give the results. The only time fuller reports appear is when there had been a sensational accident and because there was a lack of smash-ups not much was written about Belle Vue's next home league match against Wembley. It was one of the few meetings when no driver suffered injury or mishap. The following week's programme notes declared that the lack of spills no way distracted from the entertainment. The match did live up to the expected rivalry between these two famous teams. The score had been close all through the meeting and it was down to the last heat as to who would take the league points. By the time the match reached the last heat Wembley were just one point in front. For this last race Belle Vue had the strong pairing of Pashley and Worswick and these two were up against Wembley captain Ron Wills and British Champion Vic Patterson. The outcome of the match was decided early in the race when Belle Vue supporters had their hearts broken when Eric Worswick suffered engine trouble and

Graphics similar to those on the front of the programme could be seen advertising many an exciting ride within the theme park.

had to pull out; it meant that even if Charlie had won the race Wembley would have taken the honours. As it was, Charlie finished second giving the London team victory by the narrow margin of 37 points to 34.

Belle Vue had always had an open policy of training up drivers and Ted Cowley was the man in charge of over-seeing the car practice sessions. Ted, an ex-motorcyclist, saw to it that novices knew exactly what was expected from them. With Ted's help the training sessions had unearthed the odd driver with potential and many supporters had written in hoping for a chance to try one of the cars. The management were rather taken aback when a twenty-one-year-old young lady wanted to try her hand at racing. She described herself as a fast driver, blonde and claimed that others considered her good looking. Belle Vue couldn't resist this publicity opportunity and perhaps hoped to discover another Dessie Mossman. Belle Vue duly kept to their policy and allowed the young lady in question to try out one of their cars. Ted went through the rudiments of the Midget Car and sent her on her way. Everyone in the pits was agog to see how she would perform; all of them waiting for her to open up the car. Instead she just limped around slowly. A salutary lesson had been learned; in future a more stringent vetting policy was to be implemented. This new policy was clearly explained in the Midget Car *Bulletin and Programme*.

Late July and early August were the halcyon days of British Midget Car Racing. At the end of July two new tracks opened. The assets of Leicester Super had now

Arthur Westwood
Presents

LEEDS
CAR
● SPEEDWAY ●

FULLERTON PARK SPORTS STADIUM
ELLAND ROAD, LEEDS
Operated by the Fullerton Park Sports Stadium Ltd.

Season 1938   1st Meeting
TUESDAY, JULY 26th
at 7.45 p.m.

LEEDS TRACK
CHAMPIONSHIP

OFFICIAL PROGRAMME - 4d.

The much copied photograph of Australian George Bevis (No 4) and Arthur Tuckett was reproduced on the front of the Leeds programme.

been transferred to Stoke. After renovating Stoke's old dirt track, putting in the entire necessary infrastructure, and gathering together a team of competent drivers, they were ready to start their league fixtures. The day after Bell Vue's home match against Wembley, Stoke launched their Midget Car season. It was five days later on Tuesday 26 July that Leeds staged the Northern Championship. Leeds were not committed to the National Midget Car league, preferring to concentrate on their motorcycle obligations so an individual championship was agreed upon for their first Midget Car meeting. The promoter at the Elland Road track was Arthur Westwood. Arthur had organized a few Midget Car races at Lea Bridge in 1934 and with better cars and drivers he didn't want to miss out on what might prove to be a lucrative opportunity. As keen as ever the Manchester drivers took their cars along to both of these meetings. They had their own race at Stoke and competed in the Northern Championship at Leeds.

With the Midget Car league now in full swing the makeup of the various teams had more or less been sorted out. Nevertheless there was still a certain amount of latitude regarding who drove for whom. Drivers found themselves transferred from one team to another on a regular basis; not an ideal situation but one that supporters went along with. For Belle Vue's third home league match the visitors, Stoke, took advantage of the lax rules and slipped in an outsider. Stoke had a tidy looking team, being led by ex-motor-cycling speedway star Squib Burton. Squib had retired from bike racing because of the number of injuries he had sustained racing bikes. The previous year he had come

Australian Ted Poole testing his speedcar at Wentworth Park Sydney.

out of retirement to race cars thinking they were a safer option. Also programmed to drive were 'Skid' Martin, Gene Crowley, Joe Wildblood, the mysterious Jock Fergusson and Australian sensation Ted Poole. Great things were expected from Ted, who had arrived in the UK with an impressive reputation after having successfully raced Midgets back in his native country. One of the highlights of his career had taken place during the 1935/36 Australian season. It was during this season that he had represented his country in a series of Midget Car Test Matches against the old enemy, England. Belle Vue fielded their regular top four; plus trainee discovery George Goodley. Jack McCarthey who should have slotted into the team was still out injured and it was doubtful if he would ever want to race again. Bill Reynolds, who might have been in the team, was no longer available as he was now supposed to be a Wembley asset. Stepping into the breach came one of Manchester's favourite sons, 'Acorn' Dobson. When the Stoke team arrived there were a few changes. Jock Furgusson, who should have been in the team, was unavailable so in his place Stoke slipped in outsider Johnny Young.

The match started poorly for Belle Vue; by heat four they were five points behind and were losing by 9 points to Stoke's 14. Heat five was even worse as neither Frank Marsh nor George Goodley finished the race. This gave the away team a five nil heat win which put them even further in the lead. It was bad enough that Belle Vue had failed to score; but what made it even worse was that after heat five Frank Marsh was unable to take any further part in the meeting. Frank had been performing well having won heat three. In the latter part of the contest the home team did manage to rally, by heat nine they were only four points behind. With Pashley and Worswick going well there was every chance that they might rescue the match. There should have been a further advantage for the home side when Ted Poole had to pull out of heats nine and twelve. Ted was still feeling the effects of injuries he had sustained a week earlier at Stoke's opening meeting. Under the regulations governing league matches Stoke were allowed to replace him with a reserve driver. The rules stated that if a driver was unable to take part in a race then a nominated reserve could take his place. If a team didn't have a nominated reserve then any member of the team could take the drive. With Ted Poole out, and Stoke having no seventh driver as a nominated reserve, they selected Squib Burton in one heat and Gene Crowley in the other. Both of these drivers were in tip top form having beaten Belle Vue's star men, something that Ted Poole had not been able to do. The replacement reserve drives was fair enough and within the stated rules; but both Burton and Crowley had already taken other team members' drives. This meant that they had raced six times and team members were only supposed to race five times! It was this bending of the rules that saw Stoke steal the two league points, finally defeating Belle Vue by 38 points to 32.

After the league match there were the usual individual events. One of the events consisted of three heats and a final; the winners of the heats plus the fastest second going through to the four man final. The final was stopped dramatically after less than half a lap. Squib Burton was on the outside cushion trying to find the extra grip

Lutterworth's Squib Burton had had a glittering career on two wheels before he saw the Midget Cars Racing at Coventry in 1937.

that could usually be found up near the fence. With everyone dicing for position Squib touched one the other finalist's wheels. Out of control the car and driver slammed into the wooden safety fence. Burton suffered serious leg and knee injuries which were so serious that he was forced to retire from Midget Car Racing. Midget Car Racing had lost one of its top drivers; he was one of the very few racers who could have taken on and beaten the likes of Walter Mackereth, Les White and Spike Rhiando.

The hopes that Midget Car League Racing would become a leading summer sport were ruined when news of another closure was announced. The withdrawal of Lea Bridge from the league hadn't been much of a problem especially when their assets had been transferred to Crystal Palace. What seriously damaged the league's progress was Wembley's announcement that they would not be honouring any of their scheduled home league matches. In the meantime Wembley continued to fulfil some of their away fixtures while they awaited some form of compromise. Wembley's Gold Trophy meeting had been a success so the cancellation of further Midget Car meetings had nothing to do with lack of interest in the cars. The problem lay with Wembley's motorcycle speedway stars. Their star riders began to exert pressure on the management; their main complaint was that of track conditions. They claimed that after the car meeting the track was so rough that it compromised their safety. To a certain extent this may have been true; the four wheel drive Skirrows certainly cut the track up a lot worse than the bikes, but it was nowhere near as bad as was being made out. The problem that the riders had lay more with their attitude towards another sport muscling in on their territory; the bike boys didn't want any encroachment or competition from another source. Confronted with this situation the Wembley management took the pragmatic approach that the bikes were to have priority. The Wembley Lions speedway team were very successful so rather than take a gamble on a new venture that one day may be even more successful than the bikes, they stuck with what they knew best. Those drivers who had been allocated to Wembley now had to decide what to do next. Some had paid out quite a substantial amount of money on purchasing their cars and needed race meetings to see a return on their investments. The governing body's vague policy of driver equalisation should have come into play; which, it was hoped,

Because there were no floodlights at the Crystal Palace track all their meetings had to be run in the afternoon.

would benefit Belle Vue. After their last home meeting it was obvious that their team needed strengthening. Unfortunately they missed out to Stoke who snapped up Les White and Stan Mills. This was probably due to the fact that Stoke were never able to call upon six regular team members they could call their own. To field a team they often had to borrow drivers from other teams. When they turned out for Stoke they generally changed their names conning the public into believing they were their own drivers! Stoke's team building was made even worse when they lost Ted Poole through injury. With no help from outside sources Belle Vue were left to sort out their own team difficulties.

With fewer league matches available drivers needed extra opportunities to race. It was up to the promoters to come up with new ideas; the public needed to see competitive attractive meetings. One of the most attractive and best-attended motorcycle speedway meetings were the test matches between England and Australia. These test matches were over a special eighteen heat formula instead of the usual twelve. Midget Car promoters would have been delighted if they too could put on such a meeting, unfortunately there were only two Australians in the country and both of them were out injured. Instead of an international event the promoters came up with what they thought would be the next best thing. There had always been a sporting rivalry between the North and the South of the country so it was natural that they should decide to put on a series of matches based on this geographical divide. The tracks chosen to stage these competitions were Leeds, Stoke, Coventry, Crystal Palace and of course Belle Vue. Coventry had staged the first test in July, with the North coming out on top 59 points to 49. It was Belle Vue's turn to stage the second test match on 3 August.

The backbone of the Northern team naturally consisted of Belle Vue's top four Charles Pashley, Eric Worswick, Frank Marsh and Bruce Warburton, which no doubt delighted the local supporters. Although the other three drivers in the Northern team were based in London they were all originally from Cumbria. Captain of the North was Britain's number one driver, Walter Mackereth. The other full team member was Mackereth's protégé Johnny Young with the reserve place taken by Harry Skirrow's top mechanic, Val Atkinson.

The South had plenty of capable drivers to choose from. The previous year's British Champion, Vic Patterson was the South's captain. The other five team members were Stan Mills, Les White, Frank Chiswell, Ron Wills and Basil deMattos. The South's reserve slot was given to Bill Reynolds. Belle Vue were still hoping that Bill would join their team, especially now that Wembley were no longer able to honour their home fixtures. One name missing from the Southern team was that of Spike Rhiando. Spike would have been an obvious choice but a few days earlier he had been injured racing at Dagenham, not driving a Midget Car but racing a motorcycle speedway bike. Forever the showman Spike had been riding for Putt Mossman's All American speedway team.

The opening heat of the test match set the scene for the rest of the meeting when Walter Mackereth and Charlie Pashley gave the North a maximum five point win. The Mackereth Pashley pairing repeated this performance again in heat six. The only Southern drivers to beat either of these two were Frank Chiswell and Les White. Chiswell and White were the mainstay of the Southern team; both of them scoring thirteen points each. This Chiswell/White partnership only dropped four points out of a possible thirty. None of the Southern drivers were able to achieve the success of these two. Basil deMattos was their next best scorer with seven; the three other Southern drivers could only scramble to fifteen points between them. The South's total points score was 47, well short of the North's winning total of 60. With two of the scheduled five matches now completed, the other three tests were to take place at Leeds on 22 August, followed four days later at Crystal Palace with the final test at Stoke in September.

Three days after the test match the Belle Vue team were to take in an away league match at the current league leaders, high-flying Coventry. The prospects of a shock away win for Belle Vue were very slim. On their previous visits to the Brandon track the Manchester drivers had always had to play second fiddle to Coventry's big names. Despite their label as also rans, hopes were high for a better performance. They had showed that around the Hyde Road track they were capable of beating many of the Coventry team, Belle Vue being the only team to have so far inflicted a defeat on the run away league leaders. Just in case the Coventry fans thought it would be a dull walkover for their team; the Coventry management invited along Putt Mossman. Putt was to perform one or two of his most well-known stunts. Perhaps this was a little unfair to Belle Vue especially now that their cars were JAP powered, which was a vast improvement compared to their previous equipment. By the time the Manchester contingent arrived at Brandon it was obvious that the meeting might not take place. This was because there had been a huge downpour of rain around lunchtime. There was no way that the meeting could really take place and this left the management with a tough decision. Were they to abandon the meeting or not? In spite of the rain a fair number of spectators had turned up. Just in case there was any chance of racing one or two drivers wanted to try out the track but in spite on their willingness to put on a show the match had to be abandoned. Nonetheless at the sound of engines being warmed up quite a number of spectators remained behind at the circuit. The *Midland Daily Telegraph* reported that, '...the thousand and more' spectators that remained '...took to their seats in the stand, prepared to enjoy what little sport was going'. One person who couldn't resist taking to the track was Putt Mossman who took his four-cylinder Henderson motorcycle out on the track and performed his well-known ladder trick. After one or two more acrobatic stunts, he decided to try out his standard motorcycle speedway machine which regrettably failed to start. In a last ditch attempt to get the bike going Wilmslow's Frank Marsh jumped on Mossman's Henderson and towed him around the track. Still the bike wouldn't start so Putt and the rest of the team called it a day. Despite the poor weather, the crowd that had remained behind applauded everyone who had attempted to put on a show. With the away fixture now rearranged for 2 August, the Manchester contingent put their cars back on their trailers and headed back north to prepare for their next outing.

For their sixth full Midget Car meeting (the fifth Wednesday meeting) sixteen of the top drivers in the country were invited along to compete in The Belle Vue Grand Prix. This was an individual event over twenty heats where every driver raced against his fellow competitors once. The top four Belle Vue drivers were joined by Coventry team

Belle Vue regularly changed their graphics to keep the public absorbed with Midget Cars.

members Walter Mackereth, Frank Chiswell and Johnny Young. Others invited along were Val Atkinson, Basil deMattos, Ron Wills, George Turvey and Stan Mills. Spike Rhiando was now fully fit and was out to show that he had completely recovered from his injuries. The last three places were taken by Stoke's new signing Les White, the ever popular Syd Emery and "Bronco" Bill Reynolds; whom Belle Vue were still eager to have in their team. As yet Belle Vue had not yet been able to improve their squad. They were still keeping faith on their two discoveries, Jack McCarthy and George Goodly both of whom were down to drive as reserves. Naming these two as reserves, rather than booking in outsiders, meant that if anyone needed replacing the extra competitive track time could only be of benefit to them and Belle Vue.

The first heat was an unexpected win for Val Atkinson who led home Walter Mackereth. There was a great deal of banter and keen rivalry between these two as both of these two drivers built and maintained the Skirrow specials that most of the top drivers used. The pair of them were out to prove to one another that they were the better mechanic and engine tuner and as such could prepare the faster machine. It was even rumoured that Val had developed something new for his carburettor that gave him better acceleration out of the bends. Also in this first race were Charlie Pashley and Spike Rhiando. Spike was a little rusty after his lay off and unexpectedly finished a poor last.

Most of the subsequent races went off without incident and only a couple of races that had to be re-run. In heat eight Bill Reynolds, George Turvey and Johnny Young came around the second bend bunched together. George Turvey was struggling to keep control and with his car heading for the fence he crashed into Bill Reynolds. Nobody was injured nor were any cars damaged; a testament to the strength of the Skirrows. The steward of the meeting couldn't apportion blame on any one driver and ordered a re-run with all four drivers. The other driver who should have been in the race was Spike Rhiando but regrettably Spike couldn't take part in the race, his place being

The best result that Westmorland's Val Atkinson achieved was winning the Pendril Trophy at Lea Bridge, on the very same evening that Belle Vue raced there. (Courtesy of Velma Birket)

taken by Jack McCarthy. The re-run of this race proved to be the best one of the night. Turvey and Young raced bonnet to bonnet for the whole of four laps and at the drop of the chequered flag Turvey just edged it with Reynolds third.

By the time the final race came around all the leading places had been decided. Even so there was still keen competition for the lower places. In the last race the four drivers were pushing so hard that they all came together on the first turn but luckily they all escaped injury. In the re-run only two cars finished, Spike Rhiando winning from George Goodly, who had replaced an out of form Lane White. The winner of the meeting with fourteen points was the rapid Walter Mackereth. In second place, and having one of his best ever meetings, was Basil deMattos with thirteen points. Apart from Walter Mackereth the only other person to beat Basil was Bill Reynolds in heat two. In equal third place with twelve points each was George Turvey and Val Atkinson. Belle Vue drivers were obviously disappointed at not filling any of the top places and in all they had a very poor night. Bruce Warburton was their only heat winner when he won heat five from Pashley, Worswick and Mills. One Belle Vue signee who did manage to benefit from the meeting was George Goodly. George stepped into the breach to take the place of Les White who had to withdraw from the meeting at the last minute. Although the highest position he finished was only third he had managed to lead home some of the best drivers in the country.

One contentious issue that was rearing its head was that of standing start verses rolling starts. In British Midget Car racing there were never any hard and fast rules regarding the starting procedure but rolling starts had always been the norm at Hyde

Road. What generally happened was that after a couple of slow laps the drivers lined up four abreast and when the starter was satisfied that they were in line, he dropped the green flag and they were off. The problem was that occasionally a driver, through no fault of their own, hung back and missed the start and try as he might he was never able to make up the deficit, especially over the four short laps that Midget Car league races were run. Quite a number of irate supporters had written to the Belle Vue management regarding the unsatisfactory way Midget Car Races were started. Those supporters who attended both motorcycle speedway meetings and Midget Car meetings saw how much fairer the electronic starting gates was for the bikes. Many of those supporters remembered when bike meetings too used rolling starts. With the universal introduction of the starting gate everyone agreed it was a much fairer way to start races. When Spence first introduced the Eltos they weren't fitted with clutches, nor was there an easy way of converting them to accept clutches, so rolling starts had to be used. Now that the Evenrude two-stroke outboard engine had been replaced by the V-twin 8/80 JAP engine, clutches were now able to be fitted. These were simple dog clutches; drive was either in or out. These dog clutches didn't afford the benefits of clutch slip, which was something that the Skirrows enjoyed. The motorcycle clutches that were fitted to the Skirrows were perfect for standing starts on the loose dirt starting areas. Under certain conditions skilfully slipping the clutch at the starts could help gain advantage into the first turns. Belle Vue were reluctant to adopt standing starts. Their argument was that rolling starts were a spectacular and safer way to start races on their track. Because the Hyde Road circuit was large and had wide sweeping bends cars could enter the first turn at full speed. The Belle Vue management had no objections to the smaller tracks using standing starts; in fact they endorsed them claiming that hitting the first turn at slower speeds was safer on the tighter tracks.

The day after the Belle Vue Grand Prix, cars were loaded onto the various means of transporter and driven forty miles south along the A34 to Stoke where clutch starts were the norm. This was Stoke's fifth home meeting and after a shaky start they were now performing reasonably well, especially on their tight circuit. They had been performing so well that a win by the Potters would see them sitting on top of the league where they would be sharing joint top spot with Coventry. This incentive meant that they were going all out for a win. Pashley, Worswick, Marsh and Warburton were no strangers to Stoke's Sun Street track as all four of them had driven there regularly. Predictably these four were the backbone of the team, and with no new signings Belle Vue kept faith with George Goodley and Jack McCarthy. Stoke started off well and were well on their way to securing the two points that would see them sitting on top of the league with Coventry. By heat four they were leading by 15 points to 9. In the next heat things changed dramatically. Not an historic fight back by Belle Vue but a sudden change in the weather as it began to pour down, severely affecting track conditions. When Frank Marsh won heat six his time was six seconds slower than the winner of heat two. After that heat the heavens opened up and there was a huge thunderstorm which flooded the track and the surrounding areas. Obviously this brought racing to a halt as with the track now well under water the meeting had to be abandoned. A general rule in speedway racing acknowledged that once six heats had been completed there was no obligation on the management to issue free re-admission tickets. Generously the Stoke management decided that if supporters hung onto their admission tickets they would be admitted to the next home meeting for half-price. Those Belle Vue fans that had made the trip from Manchester were told that if they too retained their admission tickets they would be allowed in for half-price; especially when Belle Vue retuned for their rearranged fixture.

The Belle Vue drivers now had a bit of a respite, a five day breather! It was during this short break, on the Saturday to be exact, that something happened at Hyde Road that eventually had dire consequences for the Midget Car team. On 13 August the unthinkable happened when the Belle Vue Aces speedway team lost at home to West Ham. One might think that this was nothing to do with Midget Car Racing. Some of Belle Vue's motorcycle speedway team took a different view, with a few of them claiming that after Midget Car meetings the track took on completely different conditions compared to the week before. They claimed that the change in track conditions affected their performance; accordingly the opposition were able to take advantage of the home team's trepidation. Being beaten at home was humiliating so excuses were looked for; blaming track conditions was an easy way out. Speedway riders often did, and still do, jump on any excuse for losing a race.

Following their abandoned away trip at Stoke it was another Wednesday night home league match for our heroes. Again they were to race against the Stoke Potters. Since their last visit to Hyde Road the Stoke team had seen several changes in their team's composition. Only Gene Crowley, Skid Martin and Joe Wildblood remained from the Stoke team that last visited Manchester. Of the other three former team members, two of them had had career ending accidents. On Stoke's last visit Squib Burton's entanglement with Belle Vue's safety fence triggered his retirement, the injuries to his knee proving far more serious than was first thought. Ted Poole, Stoke's other absentee driver had rolled his Midget at Stoke's second meeting. His broken shoulder was taking a lot longer to heal than was first diagnosed. Stoke's three new signings were extremely fast and capable drivers; namely Les White, Stan Mills and Lane White. Stoke had benefitted from Wembley leaving from the league having captured Les White. A further astute signing had been that of Stan Mills. Stan had been attached to Lea Bridge and when they closed down he preferred to join Stoke rather than move to Crystal Palace with the rest of the Lea Bridge team. The third newcomer to the team, Lane White, was the older brother of Les. Lane had been involved with Midget Car Racing for the past three years and together with the rest of the White family, he had accompanied brother Les to the many tracks that they visited. It was only a few weeks before that Lane had made his sensational debut for Stoke at Coventry. Since then he had come on in leaps and bounds and could beat many an established star. The home team were still searching around for a couple of experienced drivers that would strengthen their squad. The Bill Reynolds deal was no longer on the cards so Syd Emery was approached again and much to the delight of the Belle Vue fans he agreed to join the northern squad. For the encounter against Stoke his name appeared in the Belle Vue programme. The team member who was dropped to make way for Syd was Jack McCarthy, otherwise it was the usual four plus George Goodly. On the night of 17 September the much-

Stan was one of the elder statesmen of the Midget Car scene, having raced at Lea Bridge in the early days of the sport.

hyped Syd never made it to Manchester and this left Belle Vue with a team member short. Fortunately Coventry's Frank Bullock was available to fill in the vacant spot. To an outsider, using a driver from another team may seem rather farcical, but this practice of using guest drivers was widespread. The first heat saw Belle Vue storm into a 5-1 lead, with Warburton and Pashley leading home Gene Crowley and Lane White. This great start only flattered to deceive; by heat six, Stoke were in the lead, heading Belle Vue by 19 points to 17. This fight back by Stoke was due more to their all-round consistency rather than relying on individual stars. Stoke drivers were picking up those all-important one point third places, whereas Goodley, and to a lesser extent Bullock, were trailing in last. During the next six heats Belle Vue slipped even further behind and ended up losing 32 points to 40.

It was just as well that before the home match with Stoke the top Belle Vue drivers had had five days off as they were to now embark on a hectic schedule of eight meetings in eleven days! The second string drivers were also busy too, as well as a couple of home meetings they had to fit in two away matches, at Coventry on Sunday 21 August and Stoke on the 25th. Worswick and Pashley were the two most in demand, finding themselves dashing all over the country. As well as the league matches they raced at Stoke on Thursday 18 August where they were competing in the prestigious Tommy Sullman Trophy. Two days after the Sullman Trophy meeting at Crystal Palace they were racing for a team representing the Provinces. Over to Yorkshire on the 22 August where they were in the North's team for the third test match at Leeds. Then it was back down to London on the 27 August for the fourth official North verses South test match.

Like many of the Midget Car drivers, Syd had tried his luck with motorcycle Speedway racing. Unfortunately his weight and size prevented him from forging a successful career.

Four days after the Stoke defeat there was the rearranged away fixture at Coventry. Hopes of a shock away win were again slim; Manchester drivers had a very poor record at the Brandon track, in view of the fact that Belle Vue hadn't managed to strengthen their squad. The Coventry management again felt that some form of extra entertainment was needed. The last time Belle Vue visited Coventry Putt Mossman and his troupe had performed there and had been ready to entertain the crowd before the poor weather ended activities. As the Mossman troupe was again available they were asked to come along to boost the programme. The Belle Vue team was predictable, their top four plus two others. It was the two others that were preventing them from being a formidable team. Still struggling to fill the vacant spots they had to rely once again on George Goodly. In the final team slot Belle Vue once again tried to field Syd Emery. This time Syd made it to Coventry and was included in the Belle Vue team; all the team hoping that he would be able to boost the tail end. Coventry were now a tough team to beat, with not one weak link. Sadly for Belle Vue all the drivers in the Coventry team were in tip-top form and they steamrollered Belle Vue into defeat. Coventry amassed 52 points compared to Belle Vue's paltry 19; in the history of Midget Car team racing this was the lowest score ever recoded! The only Belle Vue driver to win a race was Frank Marsh, when in heat nine he beat Coventry's Johnny Young and 'Buster' Bladon. The only other driver in the Belle Vue team to finish in front of a Coventry driver was Eric Worswick, when he succeeded to finish second in front of Frank Chiswell in heat five and Val Atkinson in heat seven.

The Coventry spectators may well have enjoyed the meeting, especially with the added attraction of Putt Mossman's stunt team; nevertheless the local newspaper were less forgiving with the Manchester team's performance. The *Midland Daily Telegraph* reported that, 'The equipment of the Mancunians did not compare with that of the Coventry drivers who piled up the points with a regularity that almost became a foregone conclusion'. The result of this meeting showed up the shortcomings of Len Hulme's Eltos. On the bigger tracks the Elto was fine, it was the smaller tighter tracks where the electronic starting gate was used that the Elto lost out. Its rear-wheel drive was no match for the acceleration that the four-wheel drive Skirrow had. Len Hulme was well aware of this problem; and in an interview he gave to a reporter from The *Manchester City News* on 20 August he said that he was thinking of working on a four-wheel drive car. There was one big problem preventing him from going ahead with this project and that was the cost of retailing such a car. Hulme had stopped manufacturing his cars because, he said, it wasn't a paying proposition. In the same interview he stated that, 'they cost about £200. I could not carry on making these cars with a price such as that. Few of the fellows who drive can afford to pay that. "All right", he would say, "build me one, and if I like it I'll buy it". I obviously could not throw money away building a car which might not be bought when I had finished it'. Needless to say Len never went on to manufacture any more midget cars nor did he begin working on his four-wheel drive prototype.

Three days after the disastrous away match at Coventry the Manchester drivers were back on their home track. In between these two dates Eric Worswick and Bruce Warburton were at Leeds where they were representing the North in the third of the test match series. In a very close encounter the North just won by 54 points to 53 and this close win by the North now put the series beyond the reach of the South. In the five match series the North now led 3-0. Over the past few weeks the Belle Vue Midget Car team hadn't been performing as well as everyone had hoped and there were still home league fixtures to fulfil. Coventry and Wembley had yet to return for their second visits, and Crystal Palace had not yet even visited Hyde Road. Another home defeat might see some support melting away and rather than risk this Spence decided to put on another star filled individual event. The meeting followed the time honoured format of sixteen drivers over twenty heats. For the event an inspirational title needed to be conjured up and Spence came up with 'The Belle Vue Derby'. The regular supporter who wanted to see their team race may not have been too enthusiastic about attending another meaningless individual meeting. This time though there was something different as Spence had bowed to pressure from outside and decided that a change in starting procedure was needed. To start the races the electronic starting gate was to be introduced and this was the first time that Midget Car races at Belle Vue had begun in this way. There was no need for the Belle Vue management to invest in installing any new equipment as an electronic starting gate was already in place as for the past few years all motorcycle speedway meetings had been started in this way.

The meeting was marred by the high number of mechanical failures which rather spoiled the competition. Spence was not at all happy with these technical hitches and laid the blame squarely at the door of the new starting method. Whether this was true, or an unfortunate coincidence, we will never know. The standing starts may well have put an extra strain on the clutches. Even so the other tracks that were using this form starting procedure hadn't suffered the high attrition that was seen at Belle Vue that night. One reason for the high rate of mechanical problems may have been due to the fact that the cars were pulling much higher gear ratios than was used on the smaller tracks. Just like the speedway bikes the Midget Cars only had one gear. The bikes and the cars altered their gear ratios by swapping around different size sprockets to find the perfect ration for the different size tracks. Being a bigger and faster track a higher gear ration was used which may have contributed to the poor mechanical record of this meeting. The Eltos though didn't have the luxury of so many gear ratio changes; they were more or less stuck with whatever their drive shafts had been set up with. A further problem could have been that their clutches weren't up to the extra strain that was being exerted due to the standing starts.

At the end of the twenty heats the first three places were filled by Skirrow mounted drivers. The best of the non Skirrow drivers was Frank Marsh. Frank finished a very creditable equal third with eleven points, the same as Skirrow mounted Basil deMattos. In the first heat Les White had set up the fastest time of the night in a time of 79.2 seconds and as this was from a standing start times could now be compared directly to those of the bikes. The previous Saturday the fastest time that a bike had registered was 78.2 seconds. Throughout the meeting all the times recorded by the Midget Cars were well on par with those of the bikes. Despite Les's good start, which included leading home superstar Walter Mackereth, he was unable to capitalise any further on this initial advantage. He ended up with only six points, his car falling victim to the many gremlins that seemed to be affecting the cars. Walter though hit back by winning his next two races and in the fourteenth heat, his fourth drive, he had to take second place behind Bill Reynolds. Walter easily won his last race and finished the meeting with thirteen points, the same as Bill Reynolds. Rather than have a run off for first place it was decided to share the top spot. So far this was the best result that Bill had ever achieved and it was just the beginning of a fantastic Midget Car career that would see him become World Midget Car champion three times. He was without doubt the most successful Midget Car driver that Britain ever produced. The reason why so little has been recorded about career is that all these successes were achieved in Australia.

Whatever maintenance the Manchester drivers' cars needed had to be sorted out quickly because the following night they were off to Stoke for a rearranged fixture. The team that Belle Vue sent to Stoke had a distinct new look about it. One great acquisition to the team was Bill Reynolds who had begun his career at Lea Bridge quite by chance. He apparently stumbled across Midget Car racing when he was delivering a package to that stadium and once he saw the cars practicing he couldn't resist trying out one of the cars. He so enjoyed the experience that he eventually purchased a new Skirrow and raced it at as many meetings as he could. With Lea Bridge now closed down he leapt at the chance to represent Belle Vue.

The Manchester drivers' frenetic race schedule was starting to take its toll. Bruce Warburton was unable to make it to Stoke, and Charlie Pashley, too, was having problems. Frank Marsh, Eric Worswick and George Goodly were fine, but they were still one driver short. The controversial use of guest drivers once again came into play. To fill the final team spot Belle Vue enlisted the services of 1937 British Champion, Vic

Patterson and this scratch team were now ready to put up a reasonable show. Stoke though were now a solid team as they had uncovered one or two drivers who were now pushing for team places. Two in particular, Reg Grice from Stafford and Cecil Heath from Stoke, were on the verge of breaking into the Potteries team. With these two pushing hard for a team place extra pressure was being put on the current team members. If they wanted to retain their status then it was up to them to see that they kept the Potters on a winning streak. In the league contest Belle Vue held their own for a couple of races; after that it was the familiar downhill performance. After the thirteen heats they only managed to chalk up 22 points and their only heat winner was Bill Reynolds who won heat five. Bill finished second in his other races ending up as Belle Vue's top scorer with nine points. Vic Patterson and George Goodly had a very disappointing meeting with only one point each. Frank Marsh and Eric Worswick did a little better scoring six and five respectively. Unfortunately an all too familiar feature of the Bell Vue team was car trouble. Stoke-on-Tent's *City Times* reported that the score, '...would have been closer but for Bell Vue's bad luck with engine trouble'.

The Manchester team now had a bit of time to sort out their equipment before the next home match; the exceptions were Eric Worswick and Charlie Pashley. Two days after the away meeting at Stoke they both should have made their way to London's Crystal Palace. The pair of them being booked in to represent the North in the fourth official test. Eric made it to London but once again Charlie was missing, the hectic schedule causing him to miss another meeting. The South won the test match by 65 points to 43; perhaps if Charlie had been able to make it his presence would no doubt have made the score more respectable.

Looking at the fixtures for August, and the number of tracks operating, one would think that Midget Car Racing was now an accepted alternative to the bikes on the speedway tracks. This was far from the truth as there were now even louder rumblings coming from the motorcycle speedway riders and promoters. Already the Wembley speedway riders had forced the management there to put an end to Midget Car Racing at the Empire Stadium. Now a few speedway promoters were turning their wrath against the cars, the most vociferous being Johnny Hoskins. At that time Hoskins was a well-respected and influential promoter who wrote a regular article in the national newspaper the *Daily Sketch*. In one of his articles he was particularly scathing about Midget Car racing even claiming, rather crassly, that the sport was dying out in the USA! Hoskins and his fellow promoters heaped scorn on the cars and no doubt this was done out of self-interest. They obviously didn't want to see their regular supporters transferring their allegiances to car racing. It was also alleged that the management of Marine Gardens Edinburgh had been put under extreme pressure not to peruse any further interest in Midget Car Racing. The anti-car stance by Hoskins was rather ironic. In the 1950s Hoskins was the manager at Hyde Road and it was he who very effectively introduced stock car racing to Belle Vue on 16 June 1954. In fact when the stadium finally closed down in 1987 it was the four- wheeled brigade and not the two-wheeled brigade that brought down the curtain at the track on 14 November.

Throughout August the Belle Vue Midget Car team had been going through a bit of a bad patch, losing heavily on their travels. Team building hadn't gone as well as the management had hoped and their problems were made even worse when Bruce Warburton decided to take a break. Over the past couple of years Bruce had been rushing all over the country and felt he needed to have a rethink on the direction he wished his racing career to take. With Warburton out more unknown drivers would have had to be seconded into the team. Rather than risk poor publicity with a poor home team performance another individual meeting was planned for 31 August. This meeting, called The Palatine Trophy, was a mixture of record attempts, heats and finals; which made a change from the traditional twenty heat formula. The whole event was dominated by the bespectacled, unassuming but brilliant Walter Mackereth. Everywhere he drove he was unstoppable, breaking track records, winning cups, trophies and championships. At the Palatine Trophy meeting he won three of the four individual events. He saved his best performance for the track record attempts when he lowered the four-lap time from 76.6 seconds to 76.0 seconds. The best race of the night was won by Bill Reynolds. In one of the finals he tracked Johnny Young for three laps; then cleverly, on the last lap, he was able to nip past Young.

Three days later on Saturday 3 September Belle Vue were in London taking on Crystal Palace in an away league match. The Crystal Palace team had been performing well; two days earlier they had come away from Stoke with a useful league point after making an excellent draw. Although the backbone of their team consisted of ex-Lea Bridge drivers they had discovered an exciting newcomer, Eddie Hazel. Eddie's official racing number was ninety-two, the same official racing number that Jock Furgusson had used earlier in the year. When he first appeared on the dirt ovals Jock had been a revelation, so it was strange that he was no longer racing. This was not strictly true for it turned out that Jock

With his film star god looks and lifestyle Eddie was the pin-up boy of the Crystal Palace team. (Courtesy of Rob Hazel)

Furgusson was in fact Eddie Hazel. Earlier in the year Eddie had been at Brooklands testing a Ford that was being developed for racing. The reason for the pseudonym was that if Eddie had been seen competing at a track not affiliated to the RAC then he would have had his competition licence revoked. With the Ford project not really going anywhere Eddie had thrown in his lot with Midget Car racing; a decision probably influenced more with his friendship with Syd Emery rather than the threat of being blackballed by the RAC. The relaxed and less formal environment of short circuit racing appealed more to their fun loving attitude towards life. One of their favourite tricks was to detach the steering wheels from their Skirrows and wave them at the crowd. Only at the last possible moment would they clamp their steering wheels back on.

The big Sydenham track suited the Belle Vue drivers and their cars down to a tee. A few of the Manchester drivers had raced there before and had performed well. For a change everything went well for the Manchester team and they won by 47 points to 25! This time it was Crystal Palace who had the bad luck and it was they who suffered mechanical failures. Crystal Palace's top scorer was George Turvey who only managed eight points. All the Belle Vue drivers did well; Captain Charlie Pashley had sorted his car out and was really flying claiming a magnificent twelve points.

When the boys got back to Manchester they were met by devastating news. Little did those who had attended the Palatine Trophy meeting know that they had witnessed the last full Midget Car meeting that was to be held on the Hyde Road circuit. A few days before that meeting there were signs that all was not well. Stories were circulating in the local press that the Belle Vue motorcycle speedway team were beginning to put pressure on the management regarding sharing the track with the cars and wanted car racing to stop. Their complaint was the same excuse that that the Wembley riders had used a month earlier, claiming that the cars were damaging the track. It was undoubtedly true that the cars cut up the track more than the bikes, but whether it was as bad as the riders were making out is open to debate. A little more diligence by the track staff might have averted the problem, as track preparation had not yet reached the high standard that we know today. Rather than force a showdown with the Speedway riders the management caved in to their demands. It seems strange that a compromise could not have been reached, but the speedway riders of the time were a very powerful lobby. Previously they had flexed their muscles and threatened the promoters with strike action. This drastic threat was over foreign riders taking part in British speedway meetings; they believed that these outsiders were taking away their livelihood. The speedway promoters gave way to their demands and halted foreigners from taking part in any further meetings. Attendances for Midget Cars had been holding up; as The *Manchester City Times* said, '...the public is beginning to grow'. Losing the extra revenue was unfortunate but not too damaging for the Belle Vue complex.

A few days after Belle Vues great win at Crystal Palace another bombshell exploded over the Midget Car scene. This time the devastating news finally put an end to what little chance the Midget Car league had. Crystal Palace announced that Midget Car Racing was to end and motorcycle speedway was to be reintroduced. This meant that only Coventry and Stoke were left to fulfil their league commitments. The league was now in tatters and the pair of them completed what fixtures they could. If every team had adhered to their

Coventry, the 1938 League Champions. From left to right Walter Mackereth, Johnny Young, Frank Chiswell, Frank Bullock, Val Atkinson and Buster Bladon.

original plan of racing every team twice, both at home and away, then every team would have raced sixteen matches. Of the original teams who entered the league none came anywhere near this number. Coventry had managed to complete twelve matches whereas Wembley only raced five, all of them away fixtures. Rather than just leave everything up in the air the governing body decided that Coventry be declared league champions. This reasonable decision appeased the supporters of Stoke and Coventry who had loyally followed their team. The administrators of the league issued a statement explaining the reasons for their decision which read, '...owing to the lateness of the season and the impossibility of Wembley and Crystal Palace holding their remaining home fixtures the Board of Control have decided to bring the league to a close naming Coventry premiers for the 1938 season, with Stoke as runners-up. If both these teams were awarded full points for the outstanding matches home and away, with points already gained, that is how the table would finish'.

	Played	Won	Lost	Drawn	For	Against	Points
Coventry	12	9	3	0	512	346	18
Stoke	11	7	3	1	404	383	15
Crystal Palace/Lea Bridge	8	3	4	1	273 1/2	303 1/2	7
Belle Vue	10	2	8	0	297	414	4
Wembley	5	1	4	0	158 1/2	200 1/2	2

Frank first became interested in Midget Cars when he saw a Skirrow on the back of a trailer. After making a few enquiries he arranged a trial at Lea Bridge and immediately became hooked on the little cars. (Courtesy of Roy Chiswell)

This final league table was all very well for the Coventry and Stoke fans but for those Manchester supporters who had avidly followed their team it was somewhat of a let down. They had been left rather up the air regarding their team's final league position, especially as the governing bodies decision was never announced, neither in the local press nor in the *Bulletin*.

Even though there was to be no more Midget Car meetings at Belle Vue there was still plenty of racing to be had for some of the Manchester based drivers. In the last remaining six weeks of the season Worswick and Pashley turned out for the North in the fifth and final test at Stoke. Occasionally Marsh joined them for the odd appearance at Coventry. Additionally there was a one off meeting at Norwich's Firs Stadium where Pashley and Worswick represented the Provinces in a team event against a London side.

Late in the season there was to be one more prestigious event; this was the British Championship. The Championship was supposed to be over three meetings. They were planned to be at Coventry, Stoke and Belle Vue. The best sixteen drivers in the country were selected, and the driver with the highest aggregate score over the three meetings was declared the winner. With Belle Vue no longer able to fulfil their Midget Car commitments the carefully worked out plans of the control board fell apart. Coventry and Stoke duly ran their meetings; being such an important event the control board no doubt hoped that Belle Vue might have had a change of heart. In the end they didn't and only the Coventry and Stoke meetings counted. After the two meetings Frank

Marsh was in thirteenth position and Charlie Pashley fourteenth. For some unknown reason Eric Worswick never took part in this competition. It was no surprise that the overall winner was Walter Mackereth. The driver in second place would have delighted some Belle Vue fans as their newly adopted driver, Bill Reynolds, was equal second with Frank Chiswell. Frank's equal second place would certainly have gone down well with a certain sector of the Manchester fans. In late August he had donned his racing leathers and rode in four league matches for the Ace's speedway team.

The final speedway meeting at the Hyde Road track was on 13 October. All the members of the Aces speedway team took part. With this being the last meeting of 1938 a Midget Car race was added to the end of the season's celebrations. The race was over twelve laps and was to be the last event on the track. Having agreed with the speedway riders that there wouldn't be any more car racing it was felt by all those concerned that putting on a Midget Car race right at the end on the season was the best option. If the cars damaged the track it didn't matter at all as the maintenance staff had all winter to get the track back to its perfect condition. Six drivers took part in this last fling of 1938. Naturally the management chose the drivers that they thought the supporters would want to see; Pashley, Worswick and Marsh. These three were joined by newly-crowned British Champion, Walter Mackereth, and popular (now ex) speedway rider Frank Chiswell plus the crowd's latest favourite, Bill Reynolds. When Walter Mackereth crossed the line in the lead it brought to an end the 1938 season. The drivers now had the whole of the winter to contemplate their futures. One driver though, had already sorted out his plans; Bill Reynolds was off to New Zealand where he was to race in a series of events against competitors from the home nation, Australia and the USA. Bill did well there before he moved on to Sydney where he was to settle and become a leading light on the Aussie Speedcar scene.

The 1938 season was supposed to be the year when Midget Car racing was to become an important part of the UK's motor racing scene. The year had opened well with several tracks committing themselves to a full season's racing. Competitive cars had become more available, consequently new drivers had made their debuts. In less than five months the whole edifice seemed to fall apart. Several factors conspired against Midget Car racing. A lot of the blame could be aimed at the motorcycle speedway riders. They did everything in their power to prevent Midget Car racing from establishing itself. The influence of the motorcycle speedway community even reached out to the press as the speedway promoters threatened the speedway magazines of the time. They said that if any of the publications carried adverts for Midget Car Racing then they would withdraw their lucrative advertising. Further pressure was exerted regarding competition licences. The established motoring press were continually warning those drivers who possessed RAC competition licences not to play any part in Midget Car Racing. Late in November 1937 one motoring magazine wrote, 'Few people would drive on the cinders merely as a pastime, especially as by so doing they lose their Competition Licences'. Other veiled threats arose the following year. 'Lea Bridge is one of the places at which participants as a driver automatically confiscates the Competition Licence, and their Licence is required for Continental as well as British Open events'. Depressing as all this may have seemed Midget Car Racing did have the support of those that mattered most - the paying public! Attendance had remained stable and as late as September there was still plenty of optimism for Midget Car Racing. Ossie Smith writing in The *Manchester City News* said, 'Everyone to whom I have spoken to seems to be very optimistic about the prospects for the 1939 car racing season'.

Chapter 7

Time Runs Out

When the 1939 season opened all the optimism from the end of the previous year had evaporated away. Contrary to all the enthusiasm that those involved in Midget Cars had put out at the end of 1938 only ONE track was left operating! At the end of 1938 Coventry and Stoke had been putting on meetings right up until mid-October; and both tracks had been looking forward to 1939. The owners of Stoke's Sun Street Stadium had other ideas invited new promoters to re-introduce motorcycle speedway. This left only Coventry to fly the Midget Car flag. This was the third track that had closed its doors to Midget Cars and in a very short time had re-opened for motorcycle speedway. In the Baxter/Skirrow camp it was felt that the motorcycle speedway promoters were deliberately conspiring against them.

All the closures were bad news for the Manchester based drivers; they still had their cars and only one track to race on. Because there was less prominence being given to Midget Cars it meant that only three active midget car drivers were centred in the Manchester area. Undeterred by the lack of interest in the North West, Frank Marsh, Charlie Pashley and Eric Worswick travelled the ninety odd miles south to Coventry for the first meeting of the season on 9 April. With no more regular team racing, the Coventry promoters had to think up all sorts of novelty events. The first meeting was a best pair event, followed two weeks later by the ever reliable Coventry versus the Rest. It should be noted that racing was now every two weeks instead of once a week, with the three Manchester lads taking part. Other novelty events followed, then on 18 June the Brandon track closed its doors for three weeks to take account of the annual holidays when all the factories closed down and everyone went away on their annual vacation. During this three week break there was renewed hope for Midget Car Racing. A new venue was to open at Cobridge greyhound stadium Stoke-on-Trent. The promoter at this new track was Cecil Heath, a garage proprietor from the same district. Cecil had begun racing Midgets the year before at Stoke's Sun Street stadium and had improved so much that by the end of the year he was a regular member in the Stoke team. The Cobridge Stadium was about a mile away from Stoke's Sun Street stadium being just a little further along the A53. As it was so close to the old venue that the regular supporters wouldn't have had their travel arrangements disrupted too much. Cobridge Motordrome as it was called held its first meeting on Thursday 19 June. The opening meeting was a team event, Cobridge Tigers versus The Rest. The drivers that made up the two teams were the regular Coventry participants, including Eric Worswick and Frank Marsh. After a successful opening debut, race night was moved to Saturday. Again Manchester drivers featured in the programme; unfortunately half an hour before the start a tremendous thunderstorm flooded the track and the meeting was abandoned. The following day Sunday 9 July Pashley and Marsh made their way to Coventry; little did they know that this would prove to be an historic day. Six days after the Coventry date Cobridge were to re-run their cancelled meeting from the week before. This again was a team event; Cobridge versus Coventry. The Cobridge team comprised of five ex-Stoke Potters plus Frank Marsh. One innovation that was added to the second half of the meeting was an amateur race and of the three drivers who took part in the race two were from the Greater Manchester area. Wilf Mellor hailed from Oldham and Bob Breeze was from Manchester. This was their first competitive race; the pair of them were behind the wheel of a couple of Elto's. As both of them came from the North West they may well have come up through the practice sessions at Belle Vue. The third driver/car combination in the race caused quite a bit of interest. The driver was Gordon Hanstock, however it was his home-built car that caused a stir. It utilised two 500cc speedway JAP engines and was four-wheel drive. In the race, Hanstock and his car didn't perform as well as expected finishing third behind winner

The All England Championship that was to have taken place at Cobridge was one of the many sporting events that fell victim to the atrocious weather of 1938.

Breeze and Mellor. In the main event Cobridge beat Coventry by 39 points to 33. Assisting the Cobridge team was Frank Marsh who gained two points from two third places.

There were two notable absentees from the next Cobridge meeting; they were Eric Worswick and Frank Chiswell. Frank had spent his entire racing car career driving either at, or for, Coventry. The absence of these two drivers was due to the fact that they were both honouring a previous commitment to compete at Belle Vue. The motorcycle speedway lobby must have eased their anti-Midget Car stance to allow the cars to race once more around the Hyde Road track. Those that were involved with the bikes must have now realised that the cars were no longer a threat. Two cars competing over four laps were hardly going to neither affect their livelihood nor damage the track. A report in the following Monday's *Manchester Guardian* said, 'Midget Cars made a re-appearance in a match between F. Chiswell and E. Worswick, which the former won'. Few of those who attended the meeting realised that this would be the first and only time that Midget Cars would race at Belle Vue during 1939.

£25

SPEEDWAY CAR
CHALLENGE
MATCH

■■■■■

WALTER MACKERETH
BRITISH SPEEDWAY CAR CHAMPION

v. ERIC WORSWICK

■■■■■

Saturday, April 20th
6 p.m.

The Belle Vue fans were left in no doubt as to the importance of the match race for the British title.

To give the cars a fresh look the advertisers changed the title of the cars to Thunderbolt cars.

As a youngster Johnny was apprenticed to Skirrow's Garage in Ambleside, so it was no surprise that he turned his hand to Midget Car Racing.

At the time there were no problems at Coventry nor at Cobridge and the day after the match race everyone that was available journeyed to Coventry. Despite all the preparations there was one thing that couldn't be accounted for and that was the unpredictable British weather. It rained heavily that weekend causing the meeting to be cancelled. July 1939 was one of the wettest months on record; it was so bad that the next weekend both the Cobridge and the Coventry meetings were called off and in fact there wasn't to be any more Midget Car Racing in July. August was just as barren a period with no Midget Car races taking place. It transpired that the last ever Midget Car race at Coventry had taken place on Sunday 9 July.

With so many meetings being cancelled and with no revenue coming in the Midget Car promoters had no option but to call it a day. So it was not the self-interest of the motorcycle speedway promoters or the recalcitrant speedway riders but the temperamental British weather that put paid to Midget Car Racing in pre-war UK. One further factor that could well have contributed to the decline of Midget Car Racing was the state of Europe at the time. The future was looking bleak as by August everyone seemed resigned to the fact that war with Nazi Germany was inevitable. As we all now know war was declared on 3 September 1939 and all sporting events and public gatherings were immediately forbidden.

Somehow or another the Belle Vue theme park managed to get around this imposition and continued to put on entertainment. Just like the Windmill Theatre in London, 'we never closed'. Motorcycle speedway meetings continued to be held in September and October, not official fixtures but open meetings using whatever riders there were available. During 1940 motorcycle speedway regularly took place on a Saturday afternoon. Because of the shortage of personnel various formats were tried, and consequently it wasn't long before a Midget Car Race was added to the entertainment. *Manchester Guardian* stated on 15 April that, 'Midget Cars are to appear at next Saturday's meeting'. This was to be no routine Midget Car Race; Walter Mackereth was to race against Eric Worswick. The novelty was that each driver was putting up £25 apiece with the winner taking all. With the war less than seven months old no one knew what the future held. Walter was the reigning British Champion and just like a prize fighter he sportingly put his title up for grabs; whoever won the match race would be declared the 1940 British Midget Car Champion. Even during these troubled times a wave of publicity went out, with the match race billed as the main event. The race didn't live up to all the hype; Walter determinedly went out to show just why he was number one. He easily beat Eric by a good twenty lengths and walked away with the £50 purse.

The war in Europe had now entered a critical phase; after the evacuation of Dunkirk Britain stood alone, no one knew what would happen next. Undeterred by all the international problems it was business as usual at Belle Vue. Four months after Walter Mackereth had defended his British Championship, Midgets were back. On August Bank Holiday Monday Walter was to race against his protégée Johnny Young. Judging from the lack of promotional advertising it would appear that there was a much more serious air at Hyde Road. In a very closely fought race Johnny Young surprisingly beat Walter.

This event on 5 August 1940 was the last time that a Skirrow car appeared at Belle Vue; it was not until after the cessation of hostilities that cars would once again grace the Hyde Road circuit. The war was now entering into a far more serious phase. Four days after Johnny Young's victory Manchester suffered the first of the many bombing raids that the city was to endure during the next few years.

Chapter 8

The Last Lap

After six years of being starved of entertainment the whole country was looking forward to the lifting of restrictions. The nation was tired of war and wanted to let its hair down and the Belle Vue complex duly obliged. The speedway track had remained open putting on regular motorcycle speedway meetings, but there was never a spot for the cars. Six years of deprivation had been a long time and those that had raced Midget Cars before the war had moved on. Post war Manchester was now a very different place with diverse outlooks and attitudes.

Motorcycle speedway racing's regulating body was quick off the mark and by 1946 a National League was up and running. The following year they were operating three leagues with promotion and relegation between the three divisions. Of the personnel that had promoted pre-war Midget Car Racing none were interested in reviving car racing on the dirt tracks. Jimmy Baxter was back promoting motorcycle speedway and Harry Skirrow had sold up and decamped to Torquay. Of the other tracks that had previously staged Midget Car Racing none were anxious to give them a second chance.

Those former competitors who had retained their cars now had nowhere to race them; some cars had been broken up and others sold on. With little or no opportunity to race their cars in the UK a group of drivers had a chance to perform once more on the dirt tracks. There was one slight problem and that was that the meeting was to be held in Holland! One North West driver who had retained his Len Hulme built Elto midget car was Oldham's Bob Breeze. Bob had only just started to race Midgets when the war brought his racing days to a premature halt. Bob was not the only driver who was to take along the Hulme Eltos; two other cars were entered for Eric Hough and Charles Gardiner. These three and a few other British drivers took their cars across the North Sea to race at Duindigt near The Hague on 13 October 1946. Bob didn't fair too well only achieving two third spots; the other two Elto drivers fared even worse, with Gardiner only having just one third place. Hough did even worse and finished last in all his races. The Skirrow drivers dominated and Walter Mackereth continued where he had left off five years earlier by taking the top honours.

The following year there was still no sign of a revival in the fortunes of Midget Car Racing. Once again the UK drivers had to look to Europe for a chance to race their Midget Cars. During the first two weekends in July four meetings took place at Paris'

Oldham's Bob Breeze tests the Elto around the Cobridge track in 1939. (Rod Pashley collection)

At the time there was no argument that Walter Mackereth was without doubt the greatest Midget Car driver in Britain; the number of races and trophies he won could not be matched by anyone.

Buffalo stadium. The field consisted of more or less the same group of drivers who had raced in the Netherlands the year before. This time though Bob Breeze didn't make the trip; instead Eric Worswick was persuaded to go along. Rather than commit himself to the two weekends Eric was content to race the first weekend meeting on 5/6 July. All four meetings were once again dominated by Walter Mackereth.

In other parts of the country there were still attempts to revive the cars but at Belle Vue there was barely any interest. The theme park was booming and every Saturday night the Belle Vue Aces motorcycle speedway team played to packed audiences. Spence was too busy looking after the bikes to take any interest in Midget Cars, and yet he did find a space for one last hurrah for the cars. Charlie Pashley and Acorn Dobson dragged out a couple Eltos for one final match race; after Pashley won the race the cars were tucked away under the grandstand were they were to remain for the next few years until sometime in the sixties they were taken away and scrapped. Luckily one car somehow escaped the breaker's yard and ended up on display at Rockingham Motor Speedway's inaugural meeting. Not only was 1947 the end of an era for the Len Hulme built cars but it was also the end an era for Belle Vue's Speedway Stadium when one of their most efficacious managers, Mr E. O. Spence, suddenly passed away on 13 September.

Acknowledgements

This book would not have been written without the help of several enthusiasts who shared their valuable archives. The greatest help came from the sons of the Manchester-based drivers namely; Lance Cooper, Harry Marsh, Clive Worswick and Rod Pashley all of whom went out of their way in allowing me access to their family's treasured possessions. The Scottish connection has once again been very active in their support. Jim Henry's, Mike Hunter's, Graham Frazer's, Del Caruthers's and Ian Sommerville's contributions have proved invaluable. Other historians and collectors who have supplied information were Colin Parker, Barry Stevenson, Trevor James, John Pearson, Alan Jones, Dave Stone, Peter Halton, Vic Butcher, Alan Bates, Robin Martakies, Adrian Pavey, John Jarvis, Adrian Walsh, Denis Jones, Graham Brown, Martin Dodswell, Norman Jacobs and Bryan Tungate. There were also several specialists who contributed including JAP engine experts Jeff Clew, Gordon Dobbie, Ian Patterson, Dennis Rushton and Skirrow owner Terry Wright. Amongst the motoring fraternity who assisted were John Maddison, David Sewell members of the staff at the VSCC library, the National Motor Museum at Beaulieu and James Peacop of Mouldsworth Motor Museum, Cheshire. I am also indebted to Midget Car specialists Andy Abrahams, Trevor Chater, Eric Walker and John Hyam. The overseas contributors need singling out too, and if it hadn't been for Gerald Santibanes and Mel Anthony in the USA plus Australian stalwarts Brian Darby, Jim Shepherd, Kevin Emmerson, Gerry Baker and Bill Lawler, much of their part of the story could not have been included. A separate mention should also be given to Brisbane-based Midget Car buff John Williams for his exceptional research into EO's travels in the US. Other overseas contributors were Lars Hageman of Sweden and Paul Hooft of the Netherlands. My special thanks go to the relatives of former drivers, namely Malcolm Skirrow, Brian Heath, Brian DeMattos, Malcolm White, Doug Wildblood, Rob Hazel, Tony Pashley, Eric Knusson, Velma Birket and Roy Chiswell. Every effort has been made to trace the original owners of the many photographs. None of the published photographs were knowingly published without the owner's consent. Those photographs that are published without attribution were the property of the late Dave Gandhi. The cartoons were taken from an original sheet of drawings owned by Clive Worswick. Finally it should be noted that the front cover of the book was designed by fellow Motor Racing enthusiast Duncan Williams of Accacia Studios.